MORE PRAISE FOR
HEARTS ON FIRE . . .

"A beautifully appointed treasure box filled with inspiration and possibility. You cannot read this book without wanting to do more."

—JACQUELINE NOVOGRATZ, FOUNDER AND CEO OF ACUMEN FUND

"A desperately needed antidote for those discouraged by the dysfunctional politics that have left so many on our planet vulnerable and voiceless."

—BILLY SHORE, FOUNDER AND EXECUTIVE DIRECTOR OF SHARE OUR STRENGTH

"*Hearts on Fire* reminds us that we need to dream again, inspire again, and act again."

—WES MOORE, *NEW YORK TIMES* BESTSELLING AUTHOR OF *THE OTHER WES MOORE*

"Vivid, down-to-earth, and well told, *Hearts on Fire* will comfort and inspire anybody trying to do a little bit to make this world a more connected and compassionate place."

—ETHAN NICHTERN, FOUNDER OF THE INTERDEPENDENCE PROJECT AND AUTHOR OF *ONE CITY: A DECLARATION OF INTERDEPENDENCE*

hearts on fire

hearts on fire

STORIES OF TODAY'S VISIONARIES IGNITING IDEALISM INTO ACTION

JILL W. ISCOL WITH PETER W. COOKSON, JR.

FOREWORD BY
PRESIDENT BILL CLINTON

RANDOM HOUSE
TRADE PAPERBACKS
NEW YORK

2012 Random House Trade Paperback Original

Copyright © 2011 by Hummingbird Projects
Foreword copyright © 2011 William Jefferson Clinton

Published in the United States by Random House Trade Paperbacks,
an imprint of The Random House Publishing Group, a division of
Random House, Inc., New York.

RANDOM HOUSE TRADE PAPERBACKS and colophon are trademarks of
Random House, Inc.

Originally published in paperback in the United States in 2011 by
Hummingbird Projects, a division of IF Hummingbird Foundation Inc.,
Pound Ridge, New York.

All photo and text permissions appear on page 147.

ISBN 978-0-8129-8430-9
eBook ISBN 978-0-8129-9390-5

Printed in the United States of America

www.atrandom.com

9 8 7 6 5 4 3 2 1

To my husband, Ken,
who still sets my heart on fire

Contents

Note to Self

AM I JUST IMAGINING IT, or is there a movement toward a more engaged, concerned, compassionate, and passionate global citizenry? Does "the odyssey generation" represent a trend that will persist and make a more just and equitable world in the twenty-first century? Is the proliferation of NGOs started by visionary, brilliant, young leaders an indicator that we are becoming a more humane and activist society? Are we at the tipping point where, if these trends continue, we will be assured that the centuries of past horrors perpetrated on one another will be replaced by collaborative efforts to address conflict, hunger, poverty, disease, environmental disasters, and climate change? I believe there is something springing from the ground up that will lead to a world where we truly are one another's keepers, where violence, poverty, and suffering that are tolerated by bystander populations everywhere will be erased by active leaders and citizens who will intervene because not doing so will no longer be the norm.

J.W.I.
September 2009

Foreword
by President Bill Clinton

THIS SPRING I WAS HONORED to be the commencement speaker at New York University's graduation ceremony. I told the graduates that I believe that in our interdependent world, the future will be forged by those who pursue their personal dreams with passion and persistence.

Of course, I urged the graduates to do that, but I also stressed that without a strong commitment to community and a shared future we will not be able to overcome the negative forces that are making our world unequal, unstable, and unsustainable. Building our own futures requires us to help others to build theirs. Indifference to the aspirations and privations of those left out and left behind, at home and around the world, is a recipe for shattering fragile communities and nations and darkening all our futures.

Today, we are, more than ever before, citizens of the world. The borders that separate us are fading; our backyard effectively stretching now through the ruined streets of Haiti, to the war-ravaged villages of Africa, and the backwaters of rural India, our home ground increasingly vulnerable to the forces that bedevil them.

Since leaving the White House ten years ago, it has been my mission to help create a world of shared benefits and shared responsibilities, where poverty is reduced, diseases are treated, hunger is eliminated, and opportunities for making a better life are available to everyone. This is the essence of what we do at the Clinton Global Initiative, moving beyond talk to action, to empowering people, whatever their resources or challenges, to turn their good intentions into positive change. In an interdependent world, these changes require us to build communities and networks of cooperation. As an exceptional woman I know once wrote, "It takes a village."

And so, I was delighted and gratified to read my friend Jill Iscol's new book, *Hearts on Fire*. In a clear and compelling voice she calls us all to get involved in our own communities and the wider world.

The book gives an inspiring array of visionaries the chance to tell their stories in their own words—direct, honest, and passionate—about trying to make the world a better place one small step at a time. You'll learn where these visionaries come from, what set them on their paths, and, most crucial for anyone who has a good idea, how they turned their good ideas into real changes in other people's lives.

The men and women in *Hearts on Fire* have used their own gifts and talents to implement simple yet innovative solutions that are changing and saving lives.

That's what Jill Iscol is trying to do with this book—to tell these stories to inspire you to follow their example. Jill and I have been friends for many years. We're about the same age and have often talked about how our time here is much too short and the "to do" list is still too long. But we're trying. And so are the amazing visionaries featured in *Hearts on Fire*. They represent a much larger group of energetic, imaginative activists doing amazing public service as private citizens.

I have been privileged to travel the world and meet so many of these men and women who find their happiness and fulfillment in serving others. I hope their work and words will inspire you to join in and make a difference in your own unique way.

I know you will be inspired by the visionaries in *Hearts on Fire*. I hope you will come away from it with new optimism about our world and a new sense of your own purpose in it.

Introduction: Idealism into Action

I AM WRITING THIS BOOK TO SHARE WITH YOU the joy and excitement I have experienced meeting and becoming friends with some of the twenty-first century's most innovative and compassionate visionaries. These extraordinary and life-affirming activists have enriched my life; whenever I am in their presence, I feel optimistic about the future of our planet and its people.

Where others tear at the social fabric, they mend; where others see the world in shades of gray conformity, they see the world as a kaleidoscope of possibilities; where others avert their eyes from the suffering of others, they fearlessly look at the world the way it is—and how it might be.

What are the personal experiences that shape the lives of today's activists? What are their hopes for the world? What are their dreams of the future? What are their fears? How are they changing the world one step at a time? What drives them to put aside comfort and safety to join hands with those most in need?

A new consciousness is sweeping the globe. Columnist and bestselling author David Brooks describes it as the New Humanism; Bill Shore, founder of Share Our Strength, describes the natural human desire to be part of something "bigger and more lasting than ourselves." I think of today's visionaries as thoughtfully and actively guiding the world in the direction of greater justice and a deeper humanity, where the birth lottery does not determine life chances.

Nobel Prize–winning author Toni Morrison, at a recent graduation speech at Rutgers University, beautifully expressed the personal importance of pursuing something bigger and more lasting than ourselves: "Personal success devoid of meaningfulness, free of a steady commitment to social justice, that's more than a barren life; it is a trivial one. It's looking good instead of doing good."

Whatever words we use to describe this new consciousness, the reality is simple: It is fundamental to our nature to join with others to enhance the condition of the human family. In Jacqueline Novogratz's inspiring words, "The time has come to extend to every person on the planet the fundamental principle we hold so dear: that all human beings are created equal.... Our collective futures rest upon embracing a vision of a single world in which we are all connected."

This book is a call to action. I am both motivated and humbled by the many people in our lives who serve without the expectation of reward. I have been fortunate to be close to people from all walks of life who feel it is a privilege to roll up their sleeves and extend a helping hand to others. Together we can make a real difference, today and tomorrow. If this book can, even in a small way, help you define and refine your dreams and plans for a better world, then it will have accomplished its mission.

In 2010 and 2011, my colleague Peter Cookson and I filmed each of the visionaries featured in this book. Their stories are told in their own words—directly, honestly, and passionately. The chapters that follow emerge from the lightly edited transcripts of our interviews. The stories you are about to read capture what we believe is often overlooked: Behind every story of service is a very human and heartfelt journey—signified by yearning, struggle, happiness, and fulfillment. These vignettes allow us to see how purposeful imagination and solidarity with others can transform the world and in the process transform the lives of those who serve.

Peter and I have known each other for many years; both of us are sociologists and educators. Not long ago, we discovered we were working in parallel and decided to collaborate on a book that would bring to public attention new and courageous leaders who are reshaping the world. This has been a truly happy collaboration.

The title *Hearts on Fire* is drawn from an expression used by Andeisha Farid to describe to us her life's journey from childhood in a refugee camp in Iran to her present work, founding orphanages in Afghanistan. She movingly explained to us how the ashes of her heart were turned into a heart on fire when she started her first small orphanage in 2003.

The origins of this work have deep roots in my family. My husband, Ken, and I believe that from those to whom much has been given, much is expected. Our children, Zachary and Kiva, share our determination to help make a world where justice is the norm, not the exception. We founded the Iscol Family Program for Leadership Development in Public Service at Cornell University as a way of promoting and supporting visionary leadership. I am indebted to all my colleagues at the Clinton Global Initiative and to President Clinton himself for showing the way forward to a world where our shared humanity is celebrated and giving back is expected.

The symbol for this project is the hummingbird. Fifteen years ago, a family friend gave me a painting of a hummingbird as a gift, because he thought it captured my sense of urgency about those things I care deeply about. Recently, I learned that the hummingbird is considered sacred by many Native Americans, who believe it to have life-giving magical powers— a very fitting symbol for the work of the world's visionaries.

Because our mission is to awaken and support your sense of commitment, we have included sources of information about employment, internships, grants, and sponsorships as well as educational and professional development opportunities in the growing service movement and some suggested further reading.

So, welcome! I sincerely hope that when you meet and get to know these women and men of vision, you will feel refreshed, optimistic, and ready to find your own path of connection, compassion, and constructive problem-solving. Please be in touch with us at www.heartsonfirebook.com and join the conversation—together we can make a real difference!

I CARRIED YOU IN
MY HEART

the
Jimmie Briggs
story

CO-FOUNDER AND EXECUTIVE DIRECTOR, THE MAN UP CAMPAIGN

JIMMIE BRIGGS HAS BEEN CALLED "A GENTLE GIANT." It's not so much his impressive stature, which fills the doorway; it is his dignity, his quiet sense of purpose, and the almost innocent quality that suffuses the entire room.

When I first met Jimmie, he needed some guidance with fundraising. I was motivated to help because I believed that whoever would meet him would be as taken as I was with his chosen mission: stopping violence against girls and women.

Jimmie has gone through a lot in the year since we first interviewed him: He suffered a major heart attack, which led to complete kidney failure. Since then he has been in hemodialysis three days a week, four hours per session. Yet he remains steadfast and totally committed to ending violence against girls and women. Jimmie loves life deeply. When I asked him about how he had gotten through his ordeal, he spoke of his family and friends and the community of caring he continues to be part of every day. His positive outlook is inspiring. I have learned so much from Jimmie; in his words, "social change requires working every day, every week, every hour—never turning off."

Jimmie has many fans and was the winner of *GQ* magazine's Better Men Better World Search. As he stirs hearts with his urgent quest to protect women and girls in this country and around the world, I hope he will stir yours too.

IMAGINE IF WE DREW A MAP OF THE WORLD where our unit of measurement was violence against women. It would be a geography of pain. We would see continents of buried suffering, mountain ranges of violence, and arid deserts of neglect. We would see a world where rape is used as a weapon of war (nearly 500,000 women were raped in Rwanda during the 1994 genocide alone), a world where one out of three girls reports being sexually abused and where one girl in four has experienced violence in a relationship. Worldwide, the leading cause of death and disability for women between fifteen and forty-four is violence.

Violence against women is a complex set of destructive, primarily male behaviors that include psychological and emotional abuse, forced marriage, son preference, honor killings, sexual harassment, trafficking, and violence against women in armed conflict.

Jimmie is the founder of the Man Up Campaign, a global initiative to stop violence against girls and women. He didn't start life expecting he would dedicate himself to mobilizing the world's youth in the cause of basic justice for girls and women.

But that's what he did. And this is his story.

An Unlikely Journey

"I have to say my journey's been a very unlikely one. It is not the path I thought I would take with my life. I grew up in a rural Bible Belt community just outside of Saint Louis. My mother was a teacher and high school guidance counselor. My father was an electrician. I have a younger brother; we were very much a middle-class family.

I grew up in a community that was predominately white, very conservative. In elementary school and high school I was one of the few African American students. I endured a lot of taunting—a lot of racial epithets—playing sports, in assemblies, and in the hallways of my schools.

It wasn't an easy time to be growing up. But I found strength in my family and community. The seventies and eighties were not times of innovation and change. My parents were very devout Baptists. A lot of my upbringing was tied to the church—fish fries, the Sunday socials, the clothing drives, the Christmas sales in the wintertime.

I was influenced by the elders of the church. It was not a wealthy church. Most church members were working-class people from the Deep South who had achieved a certain degree of security. They were very proud people.

It was an environment of affirmation. When I would do well in school or win certain contests or get on the dean's list, I vividly remember members of the church—many of them have passed away—discreetly handing me a crumpled-up five-dollar bill, slipping it to me as a token of their support. People would come to me after church saying, "Jimmie, we're proud of you."

The community had an investment in me succeeding. I am sure other young people my age in the church felt the same way. But it came across in a very personalized way. I grew up wanting to be a doctor. I volunteered at a local hospital in high school.

The goal was to get me to college and to excel. My belief system was influenced by the Southern Baptist tradition, the African American community, and my family. But I was also influenced by reacting to the sometimes hostile environment in which I grew up. I realized it was better not to judge people based on their skin color, ethnicity, religion, economic background, or physical or mental challenges.

I always had to go for the underdog. I guess I felt disenfranchised; I felt a kinship with other people who were disenfranchised. The kids who were poor, whether they were black or white, the kids who were in the special education program who had physical or mental disabilities or challenges— I always felt a kinship with them and would stand up for them when an opportunity presented itself. I always wanted to stand up for those who didn't have a voice.

My heroes growing up were writers like James Baldwin, Alice Walker, Maya Angelou, and John Steinbeck. Today, my heroes are somewhat different. One of my heroes has been my father. He was a constant hero throughout my life.

I would also have to say that my heroes include the everyday people

I've met: the people whose names will never be in any books or in a news program; the people who have been sexually assaulted or raped, and endure and survive—they go on living, they carry on hope and faith; the women I met in the Congo over the last several years who, in spite of the tragedy they endured, have not given up on us, on humanity, on themselves.

I had the opportunity to go to Morehouse College in Atlanta, Georgia. Morehouse is a historically black all-male college with a long tradition of leadership. Martin Luther King, Jr., went there. Spike Lee went there. Some of today's most prominent financial and political leaders went to Morehouse.

College had a tremendous impact on me in ways I didn't recognize until later. I majored in philosophy and biology. But things really started to change my junior year. I had the opportunity to go overseas in 1989 and study, thanks to a [Philip] Merrill Fellowship. I spent a year and a half in Vienna, Austria.

It was a momentous time to be in Europe. I was there when the Berlin Wall came down. I was in Prague when their revolution occurred; I was in Hungary during their revolution.

It really energized me in a way that I didn't recognize at first. I had always been a good writer and people said, "Jimmie, why don't you pursue writing?" But I'd never thought about writing as a career option for me. I didn't see how I could make a living. And coming from the family I did, there was so much invested in me becoming a doctor. I would have been the first one in my family to go to medical school.

But after traveling and seeing what I saw in Europe, I fell in love with exploring new cultures, hearing new languages, speaking new languages, and—you know—having the gift of sharing stories with people. After my junior year, I went back to college and finished my senior year at Morehouse. I resolved to take a new path for myself.

"You Must Pass These Stories On"

I knew I wasn't going to be a doctor, but I didn't tell my parents until after college. I'll never forget how it happened. The day I graduated we went out to dinner with the whole family and over dinner I said, "I'm not gonna become a doctor. I'm gonna become a writer." Let's just say it was a very rough few months after that. It was a difficult time period for me and them.

But my adventure had begun.

After college I spent the next year and a half waiting tables and tending bar, because I had never taken a journalism or a writing class in my life. I spent a few months unloading trucks for UPS just to earn money. All the while I was sending off query letters to editors in New York, not understanding the process, not having clips to show. Finally, a friend of mine was moving to Washington, D.C. He invited me to come with him. So I said, "Let's go for it." I got a job in the mailroom of *The Washington Post*. That's how I broke into journalism.

In 1992 I wrote an op-ed for the *Post* about the impact of hip-hop music on the iconography of Malcolm X. It was the same year that Spike Lee's film about him came out.

From *The Washington Post* I moved to New York City, where I spent time writing for *The Village Voice* on a fellowship. I felt like I was becoming a journalist, because I had the opportunity to write about more serious subjects like politics and social affairs, rather than arts and culture.

I then went to *Life* magazine. I was at *Life* for four and a half years. I worked with some of the world's best photojournalists, including Gordon Parks, Derek Hudson, and Donna Ferrato. It was the best education I could have had. I learned from people who define what journalism is today.

When I was working at *Life*, my focus became honed, because without being conscious of it I was being drawn to stories that dealt with women and children. My first story for *Life* was a yearlong investigation of the impact of Gulf War syndrome on the families of soldiers who served in the first Gulf War. That story led to pieces on child labor in India and Pakistan and then to stories on child abuse deaths and the phenomenon of the abandonment of newborn babies. That led to stories on the displaced children of Rwanda.

I was drawn to these stories. I would joke with my colleagues, "Why am I getting all these depressing stories about kids in need, kids in crisis?" But then an editor said to me, "Jimmie, you're getting these stories because you're good at them, because you're able to do something which many journalists can't do, which is to document the lives of young people and children in a respectful and authentic way. Kids feel comfortable talking to you, and you're able to convey their stories in a form that resonates with readers."

I recognized where my heart was focused—on the lives of the voiceless and people who are not always respected.

One of the last things I did before leaving *Life* was to go with a photographer to the Democratic Republic of the Congo, which had been engaged in a decade-long civil war between longtime dictator Mobutu Sese Seko and a rebel leader called Laurent Kabila. Many of Kabila's foot soldiers were children. At that time no one was really talking about child soldiers. I was transformed by what I saw: Boys and girls—eight, nine, and ten years old—were wearing camouflage uniforms and carrying automatic rifles. They were killing other kids, killing adults, and risking their lives for a cause they didn't understand.

I had done stories as a freelancer and for *Life* about juvenile violence in the United States. I looked particularly at gang culture, the drug life, and the impact of urban violence on those who are not involved in the violence—the mothers left behind, the small children, the families that had to deal with shootouts or drug dealing on the corners or were just living in a hostile situation. So I was better prepared than I realized to go to central Africa and look at the issue of child soldiers.

After that first trip, I knew that one story was not going to be enough for me.

I spent the next seven years traveling the world to different war zones. I went to the West Bank, the Gaza Strip, Colombia, Afghanistan, and Sri Lanka. I went back to Rwanda and spoke to the survivors of the genocide as well as the perpetrators. I went to northern Uganda to talk to parents and kids who had been abducted.

During this period I was also going through a painful personal conflict. I'd met a woman while I was at *Life*; we'd fallen in love, gotten married, and had a daughter named Mariella. My wife was a wonderful person but our marriage suffered because consciously and subconsciously I made the choice to put work first. That's something I have deep regrets about. To ask someone to wait for you when you are going places where you might not come back alive is not fair, no matter how great a person they are.

During this time, I was plagued by what I'd seen. I'd seen people killed. I nearly had been killed myself. I had internalized some of the worst stories imaginable. It had taken a toll on my soul. I hit a block. I wasn't able to work and had to take time off because of post-traumatic stress disorder (PTSD). I reached a point where I couldn't sleep and was having nightmares.

It was a challenge to finish the child soldier project. Once I became the father of Mariella, it all became more personal. I saw my own child in the faces of the children I was writing about. But I did finish. My book, *Innocents Lost: When Child Soldiers Go to War*, was published in 2005. It is my

proudest professional achievement. I became an authority on child soldiers and kids affected by war. No one had ever looked at the issue through personal narrative. I started traveling more and talking at schools, colleges, conferences, and the United Nations.

I traveled to Uganda, where an elderly man said to me, "If a dying person tells you their story and you don't pass it on, you'll be haunted." Well, I'm

"You cannot read anything I have written, Mariella, of course. It will be some years till your judgment of me as a father, as a man, comes to maturity—when these struggles and sacrifices are put into context. When that time comes, please know that I tried to be the best that I could—though I faltered sometimes—that I wanted to make a better world not just for my daughter, but for all the daughters and sons of all the fathers and mothers; that I carried you in my heart everywhere I went; that when I walked through refugee camps, hospitals, schools and saw curious child fighters, I saw you. You were with me everywhere. And seeing you, knowing my love for you, I held to the faith that a world could exist where I would want you to live, where men stand up for the women they love."

—A letter from Jimmie Briggs to his daughter

haunted to this day. I continue passing on the stories, partly in the hope that one day I can actually sleep through a night and partly in the hope that I can energize people to do something about this issue or some other challenge they are facing in their lives.

During the course of my work I was drawn to another issue—the violence against girls and women in conflict. I had met a number of girl soldiers. I also had met a number of women and girls who had been raped and assaulted. In Rwanda, ten years after the genocide, I was talking with a young Tutsi woman who had survived. During the genocide she had been fourteen years old. Her parents had been killed, and she had been gang-raped by Hutu militia. She had AIDS and was in the process of dying.

As I was talking with her, I started seeing my daughter's face. I started to cry. I remember telling myself, *This is where I'm headed next—I have to tell these stories.*

I started to work on a book, looking at rape as a weapon of war around the world. I wanted to do something else with my life. But I also had to honor those people in the Congo. I had to honor my own loss. I worked on the book for two years. My mother once said to me, "Jimmie, you're very strong to do this. But no one here cares." Initially, when she said that, I was deeply hurt. But over time I recognized she was right.

Eventually, I burned out. I couldn't carry these emotional stories any more. I asked myself, *What can I do with my life?*

We Are the Other

As I started thinking about my life, I had an epiphany that led me to the founding of Man Up. My vision was to create an initiative that would engage young people around the world to stop violence against women and girls. The tools of engagement would be the arts, sports, and technology. We'd use these tools to attract young people to the issue but also to teach them and to empower them to go back to their communities and to use these tools to change people's lives.

In looking back at my life, it's not surprising I started working on gender issues. From the very beginning, I was blessed to have incredibly strong women in my life. My mother, grandmother, and great-grandmother challenged me to carry myself with integrity and love.

In the summer of 2010 we mounted our first Young Leaders Summit. At the summit two hundred young men and women from fifty countries came

together to discuss ways to address violence against girls and women in their communities. We have workshops in other parts of the world, so that young people can come together to strategize, share lessons learned, and move forward collectively across national boundaries.

For example, in Rio de Janeiro, Brazil, young people are using art and hip-hop to raise awareness against violence. They're creating murals; they're conducting workshops to educate themselves, to understand how violence against women affects everyone in the community. In Haiti, we are creating a peer counseling network, so when a Haitian youth is assaulted they can go for mental health support. In Uganda, young people are using break dancing and hip-hop to raise awareness.

It is important not to look at service as an occasional opportunity. We are the other. Violence against women is an issue not just in the Congo; it is an issue in this country as well. I don't think I can single-handedly change the world, but I do have a gift. I have a blessing. I can write. I can listen. I can pass on stories. I am a messenger. To paraphrase James Baldwin, the older generation has a responsibility to pass on the evidence of its lives, successes, tragedies, and hopes.

Anyone who knows me knows I'm the guy who always goes for it. I always have to go big, and I feel that violence against women is a big issue. We have to reach people where they are. We already have thousands on our Facebook page. They're on our website. They're emailing back and forth. They're blogging about the need for this campaign. They're talking about what they're doing in their communities. Man Up is a youth-led movement. It's going to take ten to fifteen years to be successful, because we're talking about cultural change. We're talking about how men define what it means to be a man.

In 2012 we expanded our leadership team, hired a public relations firm, and formed a partnership with the School of International and Public Affairs at Columbia University. We have an emerging relationship with Women and Girls Lead to increase public awareness and provide exposure to our youth delegates. On March 8, International Women's Rights Day, we mounted a highly successful photo exhibition and auction. Since then, we've done online film screenings and are co-sponsoring a domestic violence awareness basketball program in the summer.

Increasingly, I realize that Man Up's role and impact will always be evolving. We're still very early in the initiative's life, but I recognize a shift in how people discuss the issue and the role of youth in effecting change. Man Up's greatest effect will be long-term, as exemplified through the legacy of our partners. Generally speaking, I think the collective struggle to stop violence against women and girls has made huge strides, but there's still a great distance to travel.

I've been doing this work for the past three and a half years. I'm in my forties now, and people ask me about the cost—what I would do differently. I think about the time away from my daughter and about the things I'm missing: the recitals, the practices, the parent-teacher conferences. I feel a certain amount of guilt. I could have had a different life—a much safer and more financially stable life.

I have been lucky to have mentors such as Gloria Steinem, Eve Ensler, and Abby Disney. They have been my guides in building Man Up. In the face of opposition these women have stood up for me. But there were definitely others whose names won't be recognizable, such as the young Congolese woman I interviewed, who lost her entire family on a day she was gang-raped twice, or the weary mother in Sri Lanka whose daughter— a former child soldier for the Tamil Tigers—was beaten and raped in front of her. Eve asked me to write an essay for her website. I wrote a letter to my daughter called "Why I Go." What I said to her was that sometimes when you see something wrong in the world you can't look away—sometimes you have to stand up.

I have been trying to draw hard lessons from the past. It is lonely sometimes—lonely to be a father who is not always there for his child, being with people who may not always understand why I'm doing this. But as Martin Luther King, Jr., said, you don't preach a sermon with words, you preach it with your life. If I'm telling young people around the world to stand up and stop violence against women, I have to do the same thing myself. **"**

TO LEARN MORE ABOUT THE MAN UP CAMPAIGN please visit:

>Man Up Campaign
www.manupcampaign.org
PO Box 25164
Brooklyn, NY 11202

OTHER ORGANIZATIONS FIGHTING FOR WOMEN'S RIGHTS INTERNATIONALLY:

>10 X 10
http://10x10act.org
125 West End Avenue
New York, NY 10023

>V-Day
www.vday.org
303 Park Avenue South (Suite 1184)
New York, NY 10010

>Vital Voices Global Partnership
www.vitalvoices.org
1625 Massachusetts Avenue NW
Washington, DC 20036

>Women for Women International
www.womenforwomen.org
4455 Connecticut Avenue NW (Suite 200)
Washington, DC 20008

>Women's Campaign International
www.womenscampaigninternational.org
3701 Chestnut Street (6th Floor)
Philadelphia, PA 19104

OH, YOU'RE A WILD WOMAN!

the
Amy G. Lehman
story

FOUNDER, THE LAKE TANGANYIKA FLOATING HEALTH CLINIC

H ER THICK, DARK HAIR CASCADES DOWN HER BACK, barely concealing the enormous tattoo of Lake Tanganyika etched there. Amy Lehman is unconventional in the best sense of the word. A gutsy, garrulous, single mother and surgeon, she has found a way to provide desperately needed health care for the people who live along Lake Tanganyika in central Africa. Her novel idea—a floating clinic—is a testament to her inventiveness and compassion.

Amy's work is already creating a buzz. She was invited by media mogul Tina Brown to be one of the featured speakers at the second Women in the World summit in 2011. Amy offers an inspiring example of what a woman of independent spirit can envision and accomplish.

LAKE TANGANYIKA IS AN AFRICAN GREAT LAKE, estimated to be the second largest and second deepest freshwater lake in the world. It is also the world's longest lake, divided among four countries: Burundi, the Democratic Republic of the Congo, Tanzania, and Zambia.

Lake Tanganyika is much more than a notable geographic feature: millions of people live there. This is why Amy is dedicating her life to serving Lake Tanganyika and the people who depend upon it. As Amy explains on her website:

The strategic importance of the Lake Tanganyika basin cannot be over-emphasized. Travel on the lake is the only possibility most villagers have to engage in any kind of economic activity or development; i.e. selling fish or produce in the larger ports with active markets. Lack of municipal infrastructure, education, and economic opportunities conspire to cripple the region. Healthcare infrastructure is either nonexistent or nonfunctional along the major portion of the coasts. The lake provides access to the interior of Eastern Congo where people continue to die on a regular basis because of the post-war breakdown of basic sanitation and public health services, including vaccination programs as well as basic medical and surgical services.

Amy looked at the desperate needs of the Lake Tanganyika region and saw the potential of a ship-based medical clinic to make vital human

connections among its isolated peoples. Today, Amy and her colleagues are raising funds for a Floating Health Clinic to travel to the lake's communities, anchoring offshore to provide health services and education for local health care workers. The Floating Health Clinic will provide medical and surgical services, including emergency response and trauma care, education of local health care workers, and medical transport and transfer. The design for the hospital ship is nearly complete.

Amy has formed a team including many local and international health experts. She has also made herself expert in the human, economic, and physical ecology of Lake Tanganyika. In 2012 she founded the Women's Reproductive Health Outreach Project in Tanzania and the Democratic Republic of the Congo and organized radio communications for medical emergencies in the Moba Health Zone in the Democratic Republic of the Congo. Her fierce determination to bring health care to the people of the

Lake Tanganyika basin shows how imagination and courage can lead to innovation and connection. It's no wonder the noted filmmaker Fisher Stevens is making a documentary about the building of the Floating Health Clinic.

Sometimes There Are Things in Life That Hurt

"I was born into a family of people who've always been active in social causes. My grandparents have a small family foundation that forty years ago began supporting small grassroots projects in the Chicago metropolitan area, as well as some bigger, more national and international issues. My father served in Guatemala with the Peace Corps in the sixties, and my mother has been involved in the disabilities rights movement for thirty years. Both my sister and brother are active in various civic organizations, serving on boards and offering time and expertise. So I grew up in a household that reinforced in me that you need to give back to your community—to have some kind of community stewardship and care about the places where you live and the world in general.

My first activist moment was when I was eight. A letter arrived in the mail from the Wilderness Society, talking about how James Watt [secretary of the interior, 1981–83] wanted to put a chairlift through Yosemite. I asked my mom, "Can I give money to the Wilderness Society?" and my mom said, "Why not?" So I went to my piggy bank and got out a buck, because I had a little wad of bucks in my piggy bank. I wrote a letter to the executive director, and he wrote me back. And when he came to Chicago, I had lunch with him.

I learned from that experience that if you feel strongly about something, you should do something about it.

As a child, I was very ill with an autoimmune disease and needed a wheelchair. I missed a lot of school. As a result, I was very galvanized about how inhospitable the rest of the world is to people who are not able-bodied. Like, it's impossible. It's much easier today for people with physical problems, although still quite difficult; back then the whole world was built only for people who walked around on two legs.

There are a lot of people in the world who are not 100 percent able-bodied. You could become disabled in a flash. Later, when I went away to boarding school, I agitated for updating facilities and making them more universally accessible.

I went to Choate Rosemary Hall in Connecticut and had a generally great experience. I wore a motorcycle jacket and stenciled "Choate" on the back of it, because I thought it was a funny and ironic thing to do. But a lot of the students were incredibly pissed off by that move. It was kind of an eye-opener about how obsessed people were with fitting in and not challenging accepted ideas. I never had that issue.

One of my best friends at Choate was a Kenyan woman; we are still close friends. I was the only person at Choate who had ever read books by the famous exiled Kenyan author Ngugi wa Thiong'o, and we bonded over that. In my junior year at Choate, I audited a course on postcolonial African literature at Yale.

When I was sixteen, I spent the summer in Siena, Italy. I studied studio art, medieval art history, and Italian art history, and I really loved it. I had a fantastic time. I fell in love with someone. When I returned to Choate, I studied Italian, and everyone was like, "You're a wild woman. You're a rule breaker. You're this. You're that."

I've never been a rebel in the sense of being an anarchist or not believing in moral rules. I'm a very serious rule-follower in many ways, but in terms of how you look…I mean, whatever—this is silly. When I look back, I kind of thank my lucky stars. I was sick and missed the indoctrination of following along with the crowd in junior high. I was much freer mentally than a lot of the people I went to school with.

Even though I filled out all my college applications the summer before senior year, I decided to take a year off after going to the St. Mark's Bookshop on the Lower East Side the fall of that year. Standing in front of all those books, I said, "God, I really should take a year off, even if it's just to sit around and read books, because I know when I go to college I'm going to have to read the books that people tell me to read."

After graduating from Choate, I went to Africa for the first time and traveled around Kenya with my friend. Then I came back to Chicago, got all my stuff, and moved to Florence, where I lived for a year. After I came back, I went to the University of Chicago. I was not a typical University of Chicago student. I did all kinds of provocative things, and everyone thought I was a drug addict or something. But I totally wasn't. I went to bed by eleven every night and had all early-morning classes. I just liked to dress up. I'm kind of a geek, you know. I love academic work.

Between my sophomore and junior years I got pregnant and had a baby boy, Max. Being a single mother was hard, but it was great. I don't regret it for a minute. It wasn't anything my parents were expecting, but it was the best thing that ever happened to me. As an adolescent or young adult, you often think to yourself, consciously or unconsciously, *Oh my God, my feelings are the most important feelings in the universe*, but when you have a kid, that's so manifestly not the case. You realize: *My problems really don't matter that much. What's more significant than raising another person?*

Would I want to change places with anybody? Hell no! I know my own life and my own issues and my own struggles. You can avoid confronting real things in the world because you're contemplating your navel. I know I'm not the center of the universe, and I'm okay with that. I finished college on time, graduated Phi Beta Kappa, and gave my commencement address. I was really lucky. I had my family to support me.

When I was pregnant with Max, I decided I really wanted to go to medical school. I had had a lot of negative experiences as a patient. Many of my doctors had terrible bedside manners. It is true that I had my whole arty-farty side—I was like a crazy English major, writing poetry and blah, blah, blah—but I had always loved science as well.

I applied to business school and medical school at the same time. I felt from the beginning that I wanted to be a general thoracic surgeon. I spent a lot of time with a thoracic surgeon at the University of Chicago. If I could be the lady that cuts into your chest and still be super nice to you and make you feel good, that would really mean I was fulfilling my task. Psychiatrists love to say that surgeons are sublimated sociopaths. That's bullshit, you know. For me, surgery is like everything else in life. Sometimes there are things in life that hurt. In order to get better, you have to do something that hurts.

It Just Seemed Wrong

I'd been fascinated with Lake Tanganyika since I was a teenager. I had read colonial African literature, such as Sir Richard Burton's diaries, which include descriptions of his experiences trekking from Zanzibar to Lake

Tanganyika. It was completely fascinating. I also knew this is where Stanley said, "Dr. Livingstone, I presume?"

It is a very mystical place. If you're an adventurer and explorer, you ought to go to Lake Tanganyika. The Congo—a country I had become obsessed with after reading Joseph Conrad's *Heart of Darkness* when I was fifteen—has the longest coastline bordering Lake Tanganyika.

I ended up visiting Lake Tanganyika as a tourist. I had a pretty crazy experience. I was on a boat in a typhoon, and the airstrip where we were supposed to be picked up was washed away. I ended up seeing a significant portion of the coastline, where people were cut off from everything. And I thought, *God, you know, the only way you could get health services to people on the lake would be by boat.* There are many medical problems in the area, including malaria, typhoid, and cholera, which can spread very rapidly. The average life span is about forty-six years, and one out of every five children under five dies. There's no prenatal care, no emergency obstetrical care, and a very high maternal death rate. There is very little education and practically no cell phone coverage.

When I got back from visiting Lake Tanganyika, I went back to work in the hospital and was covering the cardiothoracic intensive care unit at night. The entire patient population seemed like really hopeless cases—people who had a thousand problems and were also quite, quite old. No one was conscious. Everyone was on a ventilator. I figured out that it cost about two million dollars to keep all those people in intensive care for a week, and I thought, *Wow, that's really twisted!* Because if I spent the same money in the Lake Tanganyika basin, I could save tens of thousands of people—at the beginning, as opposed to the end, of their lives. It just seemed wrong.

After a while I got sick again myself. The disease I'd had came back in my right arm, so I had to have surgery. In the process I got injured and ended up with a very difficult side effect called reflex sympathetic dystrophy. I went to physical therapy for two years and completely retrained my arm. But as I worked on getting my arm stronger, I asked myself, "What are you going to do with your life?" I decided I was really going to pursue this idea that I'd had about health and Lake Tanganyika.

When I recovered, I went back to Lake Tanganyika; I had to become completely grounded in the reality. I traveled around the lake, attempting to learn absolutely everything I could, making friends with everyone. I learned about shipbuilding, I learned about the port system, I learned about local politics. I started reading. I reacquainted myself with some of the environmental, ecological, and biological issues. I followed every thread of every suggestion. I had the Lake Tanganyika brain birth. I started homing in and realizing the connections that had to be capitalized on. I got people to help me. And I was able to package all the information and all the connections and was building those consistently.

As I worked on the health issues affecting the lives of the people living near the lake, I realized that so many of the issues facing people were interconnected. Unclean water, for instance, causes serious health problems; we need to solve that problem if people are to be healthy. Heath care is a means to an end, not an end in and of itself. Typical measures of progress and success may or may not factor in. A great development may not reveal itself as such immediately. Sometimes these things take time.

I actually think good old practice and hard work is really undervalued in the world. And yes, I have a lot of passion. If you're a dilettante with passion, you may be inspired, but you don't do the work. What made my project move forward was not that I said, "Lake Tanganyika is the most important place on earth. Everyone, you must believe me!" It's that I did all the methodical stuff to build a case. That part is not sexy; it's just discipline.

A lot of things are like that. You can be naturally talented at certain things, but if you don't practice and you don't have discipline, you are not going to bring those things to fruition in some important way. If you are a diligent, good person, you can often do way more in this world than airy people who seem like they're so good at doing stuff, or they seem so articulate, or they know this or they know that.

It's sort of a little dirty secret In surgical residency that a lot of people prefer students who come from state schools to those that come from Harvard or fancy super-pedigreed places, because a lot of people from the "best" schools have a sense of entitlement about what the world owes them, not what they owe the world. People who really work hard in environments that don't necessarily give them much support are the resident workhorses. Those are the ones who don't complain, because they have a goal and they work to achieve it.

The whole journey for me has been long and strange and wonderful. Lots of "kismet" and just following threads to interesting and fruitful destinations. A good example of this serendipity is how we connected with the naval architect and engineering firm that is designing our hospital ship. Through a talk I gave at my old business school, retired Admiral James "Ace" Lyons found out about our work and connected me to the firm that is drawing up the final plans.

The biggest lesson? *Patience.* Not in the sense of standing by and not doing anything while you wait, but the need to always be working, with solid ideas and directions, and with flexibility, perseverance, and openness. If we are able to work with others and really feel the world around us without passing judgment, and learn whatever we need to learn, we can make a difference and make a lasting contribution. "

TO LEARN MORE ABOUT THE LAKE
TANGANYIKA FLOATING HEALTH CLINIC
please visit:

>Lake Tanganyika Floating Health Clinic
http://floatingclinic.org
1646 N. Leavitt Street
Chicago, IL 60647

OTHER ORGANIZATIONS PROVIDING HEALTH
CARE IN CENTRAL AFRICA:

>Doctors Without Borders
www.doctorswithoutborders.org
333 Seventh Avenue (2nd Floor)
New York, NY 10001

>Health Right International
www.healthright.org
80 Maiden Lane
New York, NY 10038

>International Medical Corps
http://internationalmedicalcorps.org
1919 Santa Monica Blvd. (Suite 400)
Santa Monica, CA 90404

>Partners In Health
www.pih.org
888 Commonwealth Avenue (3rd Floor)
Boston, MA 02215

IN THE SPIRIT
OF THE GENERATION
the
Medic Mobile
story

JOSH NESBIT, ISAAC HOLEMAN, NADIM MAHMUD—CO-FOUNDERS, MEDIC MOBILE

THE POWER OF THREE: Josh Nesbit, Isaac Holeman, and Nadim Mahmud. Their story captures the energy of a generation. It is all about connections: connections with others and connecting technology with social innovation to impact lives—even save lives—in any corner of the world.

Josh and Nadim met at Stanford University when Josh was an undergrad and Nadim was in medical school. Connecting online with Isaac at Lewis & Clark College in Portland, Oregon, they found the three of them shared a common interest in the developing world, and together they completed the skill set they needed to connect technology with service and launched Medic Mobile in 2009.

I AM THRILLED BY THE PROGRESS Josh, Isaac, and Nadim have made. Today there are more than 6,000 health workers using Medic Mobile technology, reaching 600,000 patients across 16 countries!

The provision of health services in the world's developing countries is a struggle. According to the World Health Organization, while the life expectancy in high-income countries is eighty years, the global average is sixty-eight years, and in Africa it is just fifty-four years. Every day, a thousand women die of complications from pregnancy and childbirth.

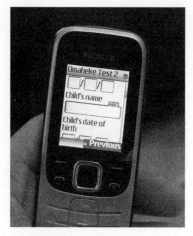

Countless children in Africa and South Asia die needless deaths due to poor sanitation and unclean drinking water.

While there has been some progress in treating disease worldwide, there is still much to be done. In the developing world, lack of infrastructure prevents health workers from delivering efficient health care to rural areas. Yet many of the gaps and shortcomings of rural health care systems could be addressed by using simple, locally appropriate communication technologies.

Medic Mobile grew out of two previous independent projects. Josh founded Mobiles in Malawi in 2007, and he and Nadim connected at Stanford shortly thereafter. They met Isaac—who had already founded MobilizeMRS—online in 2008. Several months later, Isaac flew from Oregon to Palo Alto to meet Josh and Nadim, and in 2009 the three of them co-founded FrontlineSMS:Medic—now known as Medic Mobile.

Medic Mobile develops and extends software applications for health care information, including FrontlineSMS, OpenMRS, a SIM card platform called Muvuku and a Web application called Kujua. The goal is to make the benefits of health care information networks available to clinics and health workers in rural Africa, Central America, South Asia, and the United States.

Medic Mobile's projects support community health workers in the field, coordinating services and referrals, facilitating data collection and logistics, and mapping health services. As the tagline of Medic Mobile says: "Text messages save lives."

Today, Medic Mobile has a team of more than twenty global health innovators: project managers, researchers, designers, and software developers. They have a new headquarters in San Francisco and are establishing hubs in Nairobi and Dhaka. They have attracted grants from a variety of foundations, including a $250,000 grant to build a customized medical appointment reminder system in Oakland, California, for underserved patients with chronic diseases such as diabetes.

When Josh, Isaac, and Nadim were starting out, the field of mHealth—a term used to describe the use of mobile devices to support medicine and public health—was in its infancy. Today, mobile devices are used to collect community and clinical health data; to deliver health care information to practitioners, researchers, and patients; to monitor patients' health signs; and to provide direct care referred to as *telemedicine*.

Medic Mobile is a pioneer in developing the use of SIM cards to connect very poor communities to health services. Isaac was named one of the mHealth innovators of 2011 for an invention that enables Medic Mobile to run applications that can be used in widely available and inexpensive cell phones.

Josh, Isaac, and Nadim make a very strong team. Josh explains:

> The reason our partnership works is that we all bring very specific talents and passions to the table, and we complement each other really well. Nadim is a brilliant scientist. He's in the middle of a dual degree, a master's of public health and a medical degree at Stanford. Isaac, who is now stepping up to the role of director of strategy, is a person of intense faith and commitment. He has a way of making people feel comfortable and cares more than anyone I have ever met about community health workers. Meanwhile, I am telling our story, bouncing around the U.S. and the U.K., establishing partnerships and connections.

Josh: Discovering the Digital Disconnect

" My parents were really a heavy influence on me. My father taught me to dream big, and my mother taught me to care for people. For a while, my dad was [U.S. senator and vice president] Dan Quayle's communications director, which I have to think was the hardest job on the planet. My mom runs ultra-marathons and is a physical therapist working in a school system. I am the oldest of three kids, all soccer players. I grew up in Loudoun County, Virginia, and graduated from high school in 2005. I went to Stanford on a soccer scholarship as an international health and bioethics major.

I'd always wanted to help people in need; when the earthquake happened in Haiti in 2010, I put a sign next to my bed that said, "What can you do in the next 24 hours?" I believe you have to maximize the good all the time. In the summer of 2007 I shipped off to Malawi and landed in St. Gabriel's Hospital, where my mom and sister had been the summer before. St. Gabriel's serves 250,000 people spread over a hundred miles in every direction. Many patients have to walk sixty and eighty miles to get care. There are five hundred community health workers who serve the rural areas around the clinic, getting advice and help from the professionals at St. Gabriel's.

I was there seven weeks and had just met one community health worker. I will never forget Dickson. He would walk forty miles to the hospital, six days a week, just so a nurse could check off the patients and sign off on his form. It blew my mind. What an amazing level of commitment, but also what a disconnect!

We grew up in the digital age—I mean, I was texting my friends fifteen times a day by the time I was twelve years old. It sort of smacks you across the face. And yet I had a better mobile phone signal in rural Malawi than I did in Palo Alto. So why did Dickson have to travel forty miles on foot just to take care of ordinary paperwork? It made no sense.

Back in Palo Alto, I had a conversation with Ken Banks, who is an English software developer. At that time, Ken was living out of his van at the edge of the Stanford campus—hacking, coding away, and creating this open-source software platform called FrontlineSMS. It was just the right fit to serve the information needs of health care workers in Africa. So in 2008 I applied for a five-thousand-dollar grant, put a hundred phones and a laptop into a backpack, smiled my way through customs, and got back to

Malawi with copies of the software. We used it to train community health workers to text message.

In 2009 I was blogging about my experience, and CNN picked up the story. As a consequence, lots of people contacted me to ask about our concept. I started spending ten to fifteen hours a day talking to ministers of health, clinic directors, and clinicians who wanted to replicate what we'd done in Malawi.

At that time Isaac was an undergraduate at Lewis & Clark, and he commented on one of my blog posts. We started emailing. He had some amazing ideas about how medical record systems could be integrated using mobile technology—he had a vision. It was meeting Isaac and meeting Nadim that started to push us to formalize and create something that could be built into a scalable organization.

We've learned a lot about how a team needs to grow: Hire people smarter than you, everybody works (nobody just "manages"). We've also learned that the best ideas have to win, or great people won't stay. Our product team amazes me. We work around the clock; it can be exhausting, but if you submit to the craziness the narrative seems to flow. I wake every morning and ask myself what I need to do that day as a way of prioritizing and living intentionally. I believe in activity over passivity. **"**

Isaac: Taking a Leap of Faith

"My parents are both schoolteachers. I never thought I would get involved in teaching—but now I see myself as becoming a professor. I'm part of the seventh generation of this great big outdoorsy Oregonian family; my ancestors walked over the Oregon Trail before Oregon was a state.

I grew up in The Dalles on the Columbia River. It hasn't grown much since the 1850s. It's an agricultural community with a large migrant population, and there were awkward experiences growing up there—like we'd go to a basketball game and they wouldn't want to let my brother in using a family ticket because he has brown skin and the rest of us are white. (My parents adopted my brother from Guatemala when he was four.)

My biggest sport was wrestling—I started when I was five. I was expected to be state champion in high school, but when I was training for the state finals my senior year I slipped and fell on my neck, compressing it badly. I couldn't wrestle in the state tournament, which was devastating at the time. But I learned an important lesson: There is no point in feeling sorry for yourself; just take a deep breath and go on to the next challenge.

The next year I went to the Netherlands as an exchange student. It was a huge experience—I found my faith and decided to be a doctor. That is why my degree was in biochemistry and molecular biology at Lewis & Clark. I worked a bit in Honduras and Guatemala during the summers. I also went to Havana for a semester, studying their health care system.

Starting in the summer before my senior year in college, I networked with friends working in Africa. One of my close friends had graduated two years before and was working in Burundi, and so I decided to join him there. I was ready to mop floors, be a driver, or just run errands, but my friend said, "Well, you've done some technology stuff, right? We'd like electronic medical records in our hospital. We could also use help with our community health worker program."

My previous technology experience involved new media tools for activ-

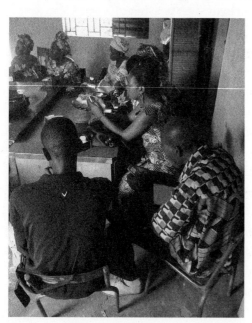

ism and advocacy, but I decided to give health IT a try. At the time, asking community health workers to use electronic medical records via phones seemed unconventional, but I got some friends together, and we developed a venture of sorts. We chose the name MobilizeMRS, submitted our plan to an online competition sponsored by USAID, and became a finalist in the fall of 2008.

I found Josh online. He was focused on mobile technology and had all these contacts who wanted to use mobile technologies to support health services. It was really a leap of faith for me to become a business partner with someone I'd met online. But I flew down to Stanford in early 2009, and we officially launched our new venture together.

Josh and Nadim are incredibly bright, multifaceted thinkers; I'm convinced that each of us could do the other's job well. But if we actually tried to do that, the whole endeavor would suffer. Understanding when and how to support one another and when to step aside has been challenging but ultimately very worthwhile. Though cell phones are at the core of our venture, we have learned that it takes much more to transform health services in very poor countries; it takes understanding the economics of resource-constrained communities. In one project, health workers in a very remote part of Malawi were using a mobile network with a very poor signal instead of another network with a stronger signal. By spending time with them, I learned that they were using the weaker network because it was fifteen cents cheaper. It was an eye-opener for me and helped inform our strategy for using the lowest-cost phones. **"**

Nadim: Breaking the Mold

 **"**I was born in 1985 in Danville, Pennsylvania, which is a small town in a rural part of the state. My parents are both Bangladeshi immigrants; my father is a radiologist at Geisinger Medical Center in Danville, and my mother is a homemaker. I have an older brother and sister.

As immigrants to America, my parents faced difficulties that many outsiders face, but also some that most don't. When my mom arrived in Texas, where my father was working at the time, they were accosted by men on horseback. To my mother and father the riders seemed like they might be the Ku Klux Klan. The mounted men started hitting their car and then chased them down the road. It was terrifying. Fortunately, my parents were able to escape, but that was certainly a night they never forgot.

They later ended up in Danville, a rural, mostly white, and Christian town, with very few people of color. It was a very accepting community, and I was happy to grow up there, but I was still no stranger to discrimination, especially after 9/11.

A year or so after the attacks, my doubles partner and I were in the Pennsylvania high school state tennis finals. We beat our opponents squarely in the first set and were rolling early in the second. During a changeover, I passed the balls to one of our opponents, who just looked at me angrily and said, "Thanks a lot, Osama."

That really struck me. It was obvious why he said it—just to get under my skin. But it was the first time in my life when I really wanted to hit somebody. And that was just the beginning of what felt like a progressive pattern of discrimination. I was accused of being a sleeper cell by classmates, was told to "go back to the desert where I came from" by complete strangers, and was getting screened at the airport just about every time I wanted to board a plane. One time in particular my entire family was "randomly" screened. For the most part, I'm a passive person, able to channel anger into something productive. But being chronically subjected to this subtle brand of prejudice, feeling like I didn't quite belong, had a profound impact on me.

Going to Yale in 2004 was really eye-opening. I learned about other cultures, traveled extensively, and met amazing individuals from all over the world. After my junior year, I ventured alone to Bangladesh for the summer. After a series of bureaucratic debacles, I landed a position at the International Centre for Diarrhoeal Disease Research, Bangladesh

(ICDDR,B), a major hospital specializing in cholera treatment, one that (during monsoon season) managed to admit more than a thousand patients per day.

Health care is simply different over there. In the U.S., you might actually expect some semblance of order, but in Bangladesh it's absolute chaos. There are so many people in the hospital—patients spilling over into the streets, into the parking lots. Institutions are forced to extend wards with temporary canvas tents, while clinicians are running around wildly trying to stay abreast of patient care. At the same time, I was astounded by how well the patients fared—in the chaos there emerged a true understanding of duty and responsibility. Everyone seemed to know exactly what needed to get done, and somehow it did. Truth be told, the ICDDR,B loses very few patients, which is remarkable given how sick so many of their patients are when they present.

After the monsoon hits each year, there is a huge spike in cholera cases. For the first couple of weeks I was just shadowing doctors and learning to recognize the symptoms and signs of cholera, but then I got careless with my hygienic practices and ended up getting cholera myself.

When I finally returned to the ICDDR,B after five days of inpatient treatment, I saw my first patient die—a fifty-two-year-old male with severe dehydration secondary to a cholera infection. The death incited all sorts of outrage amongst the staff. Why didn't the family bring him in sooner? Why did they wait for three days after the diarrhea started? The answer was: a communication breakdown. The family simply didn't know that these services were available in the capital, and by the time they found out through word of mouth, it was too late. This was a tragic death, one that could have easily been prevented, and it stuck with me.

I met Josh at a place called Pluto's in downtown Palo Alto. We chatted about what he had done in Malawi, and I told him about the cholera cases and the communication breakdowns I'd seen in Dhaka. I immediately saw how his work could apply to Bangladesh, and it felt like it was a really significant opportunity to effect some meaningful change.

After we connected with Isaac online and had him fly in to Stanford for our first in-person meeting, we all saw the potential to start something bigger. The rest is (recent) history. I am very, very busy. I am completing my medical residency at Stanford University during the week, and on weekends I travel to our new office in San Francisco to work with the team, write grants, and help us stay focused. I am also deeply engaged with our funded project in Oakland, where so many children and adults suffer from diabetes and other chronic diseases; there is a huge need for medical communication in impoverished neighborhoods because so many patients have complex prescriptions that need monitoring on a daily basis.

Our work in Bangladesh is also expanding. We are sending two of our new Fellows to work with the Hope Foundation for Women and Children of Bangladesh for three months. They will set up a system designed to improve prenatal care and encourage women to deliver their babies in the presence of trained health professionals. This will dramatically reduce infant mortality in the region.

Being this active can be exhausting, but I know it is what I am meant to be doing right now.

What does it all mean? I think it shows that once you break the mold, the possibilities are infinite. "

Geeks and Goodness

Josh, Isaac, Nadim, and the rest of the Medic Mobile team share a dream: to revolutionize health care around the world. Each one of them is a gifted, dedicated social innovator; together they are a force of real change. They show what the power of teamwork can accomplish. And they are enlisting technology in their cause. As Isaac puts it:

It's really about tinkering. Our projects work when we are able to have a relationship with the person we are working with. Technology in the developing world has a cultural role to play, a lot like the automobile in North America—it's just cool. What makes it really interesting is meeting all these people where I get to basically be a geek—where there is kind of a geek culture—tinkering and inventing in an entrepreneurial atmosphere. Everywhere we work, these new technologies are part of a new lifestyle. For many people a mobile phone is their first access to mobility, their first camera, and their first access to Google. It's their first direct experience using electricity. It's transforming things in an incredible way. Phones are so sexy!

Josh is driven by a passion for universal health:

I have crazy dreams. There are ten million health workers around the world. Imagine if 100 percent of them had a way to communicate with their nearest health clinic? That would transform health care around the world. Crazy? Maybe. But we are going to get there, for sure.

And Nadim sees unlimited possibilities:

The entrepreneurial culture has focused in on the Bay Area. It's no coincidence that Google is there, that Facebook is there—all these huge social media ventures, they know that's the place to go. It's attracting a lot of young creative minds who have a predilection to think laterally, to believe that a person can have an impact right now, regardless of age or circumstance. That's the spirit upon which Medic Mobile was founded, and that same spirit is going to incontrovertibly revolutionize the way that health care is enacted across the globe.

TO LEARN MORE ABOUT MEDIC MOBILE
please visit:

>Medic Mobile
http:/medicmobile.org
144 2nd Street (lower level)
San Francisco, CA 94105

OTHER ORGANIZATIONS DELIVERING TWENTY-FIRST-CENTURY HEALTH SERVICES INTERNATIONALLY:

>Global Health Delivery Project at Harvard University
http://globalhealthdelivery.org
1639 Tremont Street
Boston, MA 02120

>Medical Teams International
www.medicalteams.org
PO Box 10
Portland, OR 97207

>Mercy Corps
www.mercycorps.org
PO Box 2669 (Dept. W)
Portland, OR 97208

>Partners In Health
www.pih.org
888 Commonwealth Avenue (3rd Floor)
Boston, MA 02215

>World Health Organization
www.who.int
Avenue Appia 20
1221 Geneva 27
Switzerland

BE PART OF SOMETHING
BIG

the
Susana De Anda
story

CO—EXECUTIVE DIRECTOR, THE COMMUNITY WATER CENTER

B Y THE TIME SUSANA DE ANDA WAS ELEVEN, she had lost both parents. She was consumed by grief and loneliness. Susana's devotion to her parents' memory was fortified when she connected to her Mexican farmworker's background through an "Aha!" moment while studying environmental issues at the University of California.

Today, her work to bring clean water to California's San Joaquin Valley is a dramatic chapter in the struggle for human and environmental justice in our own backyard.

THE DRINKING WATER IN THE SAN JOAQUIN VALLEY is the worst in California, due to the pollution of the groundwater by decades of intensive use of fertilizers and pesticides, as well as the massive influx of animal factories in the region. The primary groundwater contaminant in the valley is nitrate, high levels of which can cause stillbirths, infant deaths, and cancer in adults. Farmworkers who live in Tulare County, the poorest county in California, suffer the most from this man-made plague.

In 2006 Susana and her colleague, Laurel Firestone, founded and are currently co–executive directors of the Community Water Center (CWC)

in Visalia, California. Susana and Laurel are dedicated to ensuring that all communities in the San Joaquin Valley have access to safe, clean, and affordable water through community-based water solutions. Since founding CWC, Susana and Laurel have become leading voices in the fight for clean water in California; they recently opened an office in Sacramento and now have a staff of seven. CWC has been instrumental in getting legislation passed to limit the pollutants that can be used by industrial agriculture, and has joined with other clean-water advocates to secure government grants for studying the water crisis in the San Joaquin Valley. They continue to fight for a Human Right to Water bill in the California legislature.

CWC employs three primary strategies: organizing and providing legal assistance to low-income communities of color facing local water challenges; advocating for systemic change to address the root causes of unsafe drinking water; and serving as a resource for information and expertise on community water problems.

Susana is passionate about the cause of clean water. "I cannot stress it enough," she says. "Clean drinking water is a basic human right, not a privilege. It should not be that if you are a person of color or low income you have to pay twice for water—once for water you cannot drink, and on top of that for bottled water, just to have safe drinking water in the house. That is not okay."

In 2005 Susana was awarded the Rising Tortuga Award for her willingness to "stick her neck out" for California's Latino community and also was recognized as one of the twenty-one top young women leaders in the country by the Third Wave Foundation. In 2009 Susana was chosen as one of four Petra Fellows nationwide—unsung heroes fighting for the rights and dignity of others. In 2010 Susana and Laurel were awarded the Carla Bard Advocacy Award from the Public Officials for Water and Environmental Reform.

Susana was born in California of Mexican parents, her father a farmworker and her mother a homemaker. Her father died when she was six years old, and her mother died of cancer when she was eleven.

We Called It Fairy Dust

"Both my parents were very loving people and always encouraged my brother and me to go to school. I never knew that other kids took the summers off, because my mom always had us in school. I am very grateful for that, because it set me on the path where I am now. I never saw my parents fight or argue—it was just this loving family. After my parents died, I focused on school with my brother.

My family is a hardworking family. Most of my uncles and aunts are farmworkers. I decided to go to college, not to avoid working in the fields but to become a voice for those who do work in the fields, so that they're respected. I have true respect for people who are hard workers—I learned that from my family. I learned not to complain about things I didn't have, so I complained very little growing up. But I miss my parents dearly.

I went to UC Santa Barbara when I was seventeen. I studied environmental studies and geography. I was the first one in my family to go to college. But I was on my own in college. That was hard! I think I spent the first quarter crying. I called my brother every day and said I wanted to come home. He kept saying, "There is no home." He was saying, "You can't come back; you have to find the strength to go on." He made me hard and very strong.

In college I was nicknamed "the militant," not because of my politics but because I would go to bed at nine o'clock every night. I was really focused on my education, and I was always prepared for my exams.

The only way I survived in high school and in college was by going back to Mexico in the summers, to where my parents were from and where they are now buried. I would sell my college books before summer so I could buy my plane ticket and go back to Mexico to pay my respects. I have a lot of family in Mexico who I love and who love me.

In one of my college environmental studies classes, the professor talked about injustices and how certain industrial facilities that produce toxic wastes are put in specific areas for political reasons. There are actually reports that say, "If there are people of color and they're Catholic, we should put the facility there, because these people will complain less."

It reminded me of how, when I was a kid, we watched pesticides being sprayed on the fields. We called it fairy dust. In college I learned that this is illegal. I was just making these connections and realizing, "Wow, I played in that!"

But although the professors and students were talking about people who look like me, there were very few of us in the classroom. I kept thinking, "Why is it that people that don't really look like me are coming up with these terms and talking about these issues? We should be talking about it. We live it, you know." So I became very hungry to learn more about the issues of social justice in the state.

In college I did an internship in Aguascalientes, Mexico, teaching kids about water. Then I was an intern with the Santa Barbara County Water Agency. I also interned after school with a project called Agua Pura, where it was my job to promote oil recycling, oil filter recycling, and oil collection. Through all these jobs, water was the key. But I felt like I needed to do something more. So I got a part-time job in Santa Barbara with the Community Environmental Council as their pollution prevention coordinator.

I suspected that a lot of the waste produced through agriculture and industry was being shipped to areas where people who looked like me lived. So I challenged my boss about the unfairness of these policies. She said, "Susana, the alternative is that people will dump in the ocean." But I wasn't satisfied with this answer. I investigated further. Sure enough, I confirmed a lot of waste ends up where I work now—in California's Central Valley. We are the toilet bowl of the state.

Two Different Californias

It's very ironic. The Central Valley is the fruit and nut basket of the world. We produce oranges, grapes, almonds... you name it. But there are all sorts of contaminants in our drinking water. The majority of people in the valley are farmworkers and people of color. When you drive through the state, you see two different Californias: on the one side, palm trees, grape arbors, and lush valleys; on the other side, stinky air and polluted streams.

For a while I lived with my aunt up north, where I got a job as a planner with the county. I did that for six months. Then I interviewed with the Center on Race, Poverty and the Environment. I got
the job and put myself in a situation where I was alone again, since I didn't know anyone in the Central Valley. I moved to Delano, where the United Farm Workers movement began back in the 1950s. I thought, *Oh my God, I'm going to be where Cesar Chavez started the movement.* It was like coming home.

Delano is a very poor city. You see a lot of 99-cent shops, and there are prisons everywhere. I just hit the ground running. There I met my co-director, Laurel Firestone—she was director of the Rural Water Poverty Project. We did a lot of work locally, fighting the fights. Gradually people heard about our work. For example, we got a call from another place called Ducor, where the water coming out of people's faucets was black.

We went to Ducor and organized the community around the water problem. It turned out that the water provider wasn't injecting chlorine the right way. The experience highlighted the need to work with local residents; you have to win some local fights before thinking big.

We jumped to another location, where the water provider was trying to charge $675 a home, in addition to the monthly water bill, for people who had extended family in their house, regardless of the amount of water used. That was total discrimination against farmworkers, so we fought it. Soon Laurel and I got to be known as the Water Girls. We formed a coalition called AGUA, which stands for Asociatión de Gente Unida por el Agua. There's a reason why disadvantaged people have the reality that they have—it's because they're not represented anywhere. The powerful decision-makers are people who don't look like us; they couldn't care less about us.

Build Your Base

After working together for a year and a half, Laurel and I decided to start our own nonprofit. We had no money, but our work had already begun. We knew we needed to form an organization dedicated solely to fixing California's dirty secret: the lack of access to clean water, especially for poor people and people of color.

We all have power. It's my job as an activist, as a fundraiser, and as a co-director of CWC to help people understand that we have power. It needs to be a win-win situation. For me, water is the most basic human need, and fighting for it is essential. If we are passionate about it and express that passion, we can make change.

Three years ago we went to Turkey to be part of the World Water Forum, and Nickelodeon News came to highlight our young people. We have helped pass legislative bills and have brought money to the region. This work is a marathon. I try to keep a balanced life, but the cause is on my mind all the time. The air quality in the valley is poor and I have had some serious asthma attacks. The doctor suggested I leave the valley, but that's not the point. The goal isn't to walk away, it's to clean up the air and water! We're really building our base.

I think all of us have a responsibility to ensure that everyone can fill up a glass of water from the tap without the fear of becoming sick, no matter who you are and where you come from. We need to go back to respecting dignity for human life. My job is to empower people to become leaders, because one person is not going to change the world—it requires all of us to be part of something big. **"**

TO LEARN MORE ABOUT THE COMMUNITY
WATER CENTER
please visit:

>Community Water Center
www.communitywatercenter.org
311 W. Murray Avenue
Visalia, CA 93291

OTHER ORGANIZATIONS ADVOCATING FOR
CLEAN WATER:

>Charity: Water
www.charitywater.org
200 Varick Street (Suite 201)
New York, NY 10014

>Earthwatch Institute
www.earthwatch.org
114 Western Avenue
Boston, MA 02134

>Environmental Defense Center
www.edcnet.org
906 Garden Street
Santa Barbara, CA 93101

>Oceana
http://na.oceana.org
1350 Connecticut Ave NW (5th Floor)
Washington, DC 20036

ALL I NEED TO DO IS
TO BEGIN

the
Andeisha Farid
story

FOUNDER AND EXECUTIVE DIRECTOR,

THE AFGHAN CHILD EDUCATION AND CARE ORGANIZATION

WRITING ABOUT ANDEISHA FARID IS TOUGH FOR ME. There is something about the enormity of her early childhood deprivation in an Iranian refugee camp, lacking necessities of the most basic kind—clean water, sanitation, education, community, you name it—that is hard to fathom. But with wisdom and love, Andeisha's parents got her to a Pakistani refugee camp, where conditions were better and where, despite being separated from her parents and her siblings, she at least managed to get an education.

Feeling blessed she'd been able to learn to read and write, Andeisha then courageously charted the next chapter of her life. She took up the challenge of bringing Afghan children the chance to obtain an education in safe, clean, loving places.

DECADES OF POLITICAL INSTABILITY have taken a profound economic and social toll on Afghanistan. In the 1970s, the country's central governments grew increasingly unstable, until in 1979 the Soviet Union sent troops to support the tottering communist regime. In 1989 Soviet troops withdrew, and in 1996 the Taliban established theocratic rule. After the September 11, 2001, terrorist attacks on the United States, the Taliban were driven from power, and a new government was established.

This history of chaos and violence has led to a society where the average life expectancy is just forty-five years. Afghanistan has the second-highest death rate in the world and the second-highest infant mortality rate in the world. Just 28 percent of fifteen-year-olds can read or write.

In 2003, motivated by the love of her country and her people, Andeisha established a safe house for twenty Afghan orphans, child laborers, and street children in Islamabad, Pakistan—this was the beginning of the Afghan Child Education and Care Organization (AFCECO), of which Andeisha is founder and chief executive officer. Partnering with CharityHelp International, AFCECO now runs eleven orphanages in Afghanistan and Pakistan that were described as "a haven for Afghan children" by NBC News's Brian Williams when he visited.

Children of War

"I was born in 1983 during the Soviet invasion. The day I was born, my village was turned to rubble by a Soviet air strike. The first sounds I heard as a child were bombs and rockets exploding and the screaming of helpless widows and children. My family had to flee for safety. My father, who had been a police officer, carried me on his shoulders, while my mother and six siblings walked with him. Along with thousands of other Afghan families, we walked for what felt like thousands of miles to take refuge in the closest neighboring country, Iran.

We settled in a remote desert area close to the Iran-Afghanistan border. As other refugees gathered there, people started making tents from the materials they had brought with them. I can only compare this camp to a living graveyard.

The nearest city was three hours away. It was nearly impossible for people to find cars or buses for travel back and forth. There were no schools, no medical facilities, and no clean water to drink. I saw many, many children die before my eyes. You can't imagine how many women died while giving birth, because there was no medical help.

Most horrible of all was the ruthlessness of the Iranian police toward Afghans. They could do anything they wanted to us. There were no signs of the United Nations or the Red Cross—we were alone.

I was one of the fortunate children. When I was eight, my parents arranged to send me to a refugee camp in Pakistan, where I could go to school. My life changed for the better there, because the camp was run by a group of women who were liberated, passionate, and committed to change.

I went to several camps in Pakistan. The last one was the best, because it was like a home. There was water, a library where people could read books, a theater where people could watch movies—and a school for boys and girls. That was life-changing for me. I was going to school, sitting on a chair with a small desk. I had notebooks and textbooks to read!

After two years I got a good position in my class: I was one of the captains. I really loved my teachers. The women who ran the school inspired me to teach other women and help other kids. All of them were so passionate about educating us, not only to read and write but to tell us what was happening in Afghanistan. I'd really never seen Afghanistan. I dreamed of going back home and being a child like any other child.

Around 1992 the Soviet puppet regime collapsed. My family decided to go back to Afghanistan. That's when my twelve-year-old brother was killed. We were crossing the border between Iran and Afghanistan on motorbikes. It was evening, and my father had left my brother and two of my sisters with a friend in Iran.

The next morning he went back to Iran in a car to bring my brother and sisters back across the border to Afghanistan, when gunfire broke out. The Iranian police were shooting wildly. My father asked the driver to stop. He was injured and bleeding and wanted to get his children away from the shooting. When he went back to the car to get my brother, he saw that my brother had been shot through the heart.

My father then brought the car to the area where we were waiting. I woke up to the sound of my father's voice, and I realized that something was wrong, because I had never heard him like that before. My mother went to the car and all she saw was a blanket. When she opened the blanket, she saw her son. She screamed, "Girls, come here! He is alive!" because his eyes were open and his body was still warm. But my sister had seen what happened and said, "No, he was killed."

They buried my brother. My father didn't see his son anymore. I can't tell you how hard it was for my mother. My brother had been the top student in his whole school. When he was killed, his classmates came together to celebrate him, because he was such a great student and because everybody loved him.

All I Need to Do Is to Begin

We went back to Afghanistan in 1992 with the hope of a peaceful life, but that was not to be. There was a civil war in Afghanistan—the Mujahideen and the Taliban were fighting for power. More than sixty thousand people were killed, and thousands of women and young girls were kidnapped and gang-raped. Countless children were abused, and child smuggling was common. Even museums were looted. So my parents brought us back to the refugee camp in Pakistan, and they went back to Afghanistan.

By this time I was completely engaged in school. I learned organizational skills. I always loved being a leader. I started teaching other women when I was seventeen. When I was eighteen, I got a scholarship to study at an all-Afghan school in Pakistan. I went to college in Islamabad.

While I was living in Islamabad, I started working in an Afghan school as an assistant to the principal. I was attached to each one of the children. After September 2001, many visitors and foreigners came to the school. We received funding, and the school got much better.

There were hundreds of street children begging or selling things. I remember going to one of the mothers and saying, "Please send your daughter to school." She said, "I want her to be educated, but she's

collecting papers from the garbage and is selling them. This is how we get food."

After talking with the teachers, I got the idea of bringing the children back to school. I brought twenty of them together in a small house. I said, "All I need to do is to begin. If we educate these children, we will give them a chance to become teachers, engineers, doctors, and leaders. They might give back to their country what their country desperately needs."

Some people from the Afghan community helped me. Some bought food. Some bought school supplies. I really felt hope. I had carried all those tragedies of my childhood in my heart as burning ashes. But those ashes turned to flames when I brought those kids back to that safe house.

Then I met Paul Stevers, the president of CharityHelp International. He had the idea of a child sponsorship program. He said, "We will upload children's profiles on the website, and people will sponsor them. This is how we can get financial support." I said, "Okay, let's see what happens." All the children were sponsored quickly. So now I said, "Why don't we bring in more kids?"

Today we have eleven orphanages, with over six hundred kids. Our children come from all over Afghanistan. We do more than feed and house them, we provide a good education. We teach them to embrace equality and to respect each other regardless of religion, gender, ethnicity, or race. They come to know they are Afghans, and I am sure democracy, peace, and freedom will come to Afghanistan through these kids.

Recently we experienced a temporary financial scare when USAID did not renew their funding of our New Learning Center, but luckily we have been fortunate enough to find other funding. With the new financial backing we were able to build an activities resource center with a computer lab and a conference hall, both connected to the Internet. We also have an all-encompassing music program for the Kabul children and a girl's soccer team! We are going to launch a program for girls about women's human and legal rights. Education for both girls and boys is very important. If we have good men who let their wives work, I'm sure change will come to Afghanistan.

In 2012 we were very fortunate to have the U.S. Embassy's Afghan Women's Empowerment Fund and Goldman Sachs's 10,000 Women project finance a bus trip across the United States for six of our children from orphanages in Kabul. They visited more than fifteen cities from New York to San Francisco and learned much about America. Wonderfully, many of our American supporters were even able to meet the children.

There have been times when I have had to explain the mission of AFCECO to the Afghan government, and this has not always been easy. But I am committed to the long term. There are lots of meetings and paperwork, but I know in my heart that no matter how hard it is we will be successful, because people know we are saving children and we are doing all we can to help our country.

I am married to a good man who supports me and works with me at AFCECO. I have known him since childhood—he was a close friend of my brother, who I lost. We have a six-year-old son together. While sometimes I had a hard time with my mother growing up—after I finished high school she said that was enough schooling—today she really respects women's education. She is so proud of my work and, along with my father, is very supportive.

Recently a girl joined us from a village where three young girls had died from self-immolation. The reason they did this terrible thing was that their lives were so tough. They felt death was the only choice for them. Lots of women do this in Afghanistan. But today this young girl is doing very well.

Another girl, Mahbuba, joined the orphanage when she was just seven years old. She is from Nuristan—an isolated part of Afghanistan. When she came to us, she could only speak Nuristani, but she became one of the top students in the whole school. Today she speaks five languages. She speaks English very well—better than me! She also speaks Italian, and right now she is in Italy on a scholarship. She will go to university in Milan.

During her summer vacations, Mahbuba comes back to work with the kids. This is because she needs to keep the flame of Afghanistan alive in her heart. She shouldn't forget Afghanistan. Her father is so proud of her. If she was in another part of Afghanistan, she would have a few children by now. Today she is a good leader and will change many lives in the future.

I have a broad vision for the future. To cure our war-stricken nation, we need to invest in children. It's much easier to educate a child than an old person. The children are the ones that will make our future better. **"**

TO LEARN MORE ABOUT THE AFGHAN CHILD EDUCATION AND CARE ORGANIZATION please visit:

>**Afghan Child Education and Care Organization**
www.afceco.org
PO Box 5820
Kabul, Afghanistan

OTHER ORGANIZATIONS EDUCATING AND CARING FOR AFGHAN CHILDREN:

>**Hope for Afghan Children**
www.hopeforafghanchildren.com
c/o CharityHelp International
PO Box 1904
Annapolis, MD 21404

>**Save the Children**
www.savethechildren.org
54 Wilton Road
Westport, CT 06880

>**SOS Children's Villages**
www.sos-usa.org
1001 Connecticut Avenue NW (Suite 1250)
Washington, DC 20036

>**UNICEF**
www.unicef.org
PO Box 54
Kabul, Afghanistan

>**U.S.–Afghan Women's Council**
http://gucchd.georgetown.edu/usawc
Georgetown University Center for Child and Human Development
3300 Whitehaven Street NW
Washington, DC 20057

THE LAPTOP IS THE NEW SEWING MACHINE

the
Leila Janah
story

FOUNDER AND CHIEF EXECUTIVE OFFICER, SAMASOURCE

FOR LEILA CHIRAYATH JANAH, social justice is a four-letter word: work. It is a message she absorbed at the dinner table growing up. Leila's parents were educated, intellectual immigrants, although her mother sliced onions at a fast-food restaurant to earn a living in America.

Ultimately, Leila was able to attend the California Academy of Math and Science, a regional magnet school in Los Angeles, where her passion for addressing the consequences of injustice and inequality flourished. It was an important first step on the road she is traveling now—providing jobs to those who have the willingness and the talent but little opportunity.

Brilliant and beautiful, Leila has created an imaginative approach to poverty reduction that has been deeply influenced by her unusual family history. Her success is nothing less than incredible and a testimony to her innovative and daring mind.

LEILA IS THE FOUNDER AND CHIEF EXECUTIVE OFFICER OF SAMASOURCE. Started in 2008, Samasource empowers very poor people in Kenya, India, Pakistan, Uganda, the Caribbean, and the United States to start their own "microwork centers," serving some of the world's largest companies. Just as microcredit promotes economic development by helping poor people finance their own start-up businesses, microwork applies twenty-first-century technology and the transformative power of the marketplace to the age-old problem of poverty.

Since its founding, Samasource has experienced sustained growth. Today, Samasource has offices in San Francisco and Nairobi employing thirty dedicated professionals. Leila has been able to hire very talented colleagues through a grant she received from Google.org after submitting only a two-page proposal!

To date, Samasource has paid out more than two million dollars to 2,700 marginalized women and youth supporting roughly 10,000 people in Africa, South Asia, and the Caribbean. It is not surprising that in 2012 Samasource received Secretary of State Hillary Clinton's $500,000 Innovation Award for Empowering Women and Girls. Recently, Leila and her colleagues began working on a large project with Oxfam Novib, the Dutch development agency. This program funds an innovative experiment to bring microwork to rural areas in northern Uganda, where there are almost no jobs for young men and women leaving high school and university. In East Africa, Samasource is spearheading a ten-million-dollar project employing three hundred people.

In 2012 Leila started a new program called Samax to fund her more experimental ideas, one of which is SamaxUSA. The first project SamaxUSA is tackling involves training low-income community college students to identify where online work is available so they can earn enough income to stay in school until graduation.

Another project of Samax is Samahope, which allows anyone, anywhere, to fund life-changing surgeries for people who can't afford them. Samahope partners with African clinics and hospitals with track records of excellent care and fiscal discipline. These partners post on the Web profiles of patients who have recently received or are awaiting surgery. Users on the site browse profiles, choose patients they'd like to fund, and donate via PayPal or credit card. The use of crowd sourcing to fund humanitarian projects is becoming more and more utilized by nonprofits, and Samahope is leading the way.

Leila and her team are well on their way to becoming leaders in providing grassroots low-cost solutions to some of the world's most chronic challenges. It all started with Leila's innovative thinking and perseverance and her wholehearted commitment to ending poverty.

A World of Ideas

"My great-grandfather on my mother's side, Sharat Chandra Janah, was born in a small fishing town in India called Midnapore. Although he was from a low caste, he ended up going to a decent British school, did well, and got into Calcutta University. There he had to sit at a different table than the other students, because his caste was so much lower than everyone else's. As a result, he always had a sense of resentment against the caste system and any other system that denies some people opportunity simply because of the station they happen to be born into.

He became a trial lawyer in Calcutta and bought a house at 57 Rash-behari Avenue, a main thoroughfare in Calcutta. It became a big extended-family compound as well as the location of many political and cultural discussions. That's where my mother was raised. Many unusual people lived in or visited 57 Rashbehari. For instance, my mother's uncle, Sunil Janah, was a documentary photographer who worked for a newspaper run by the Communist Party of India for some time. He traveled with Gandhi, P. C. Joshi, and a number of political leaders, photographing their amazing lives. He also was the first prominent South Asian photographer to document the lives of Adivasis, India's indigenous people.

My mother's mother, Christiane Zeebroek, was an intrepid Belgian woman whose house in Brussels was occupied by the Nazis in World War II. Her family was so shaken by that experience that they fled by caravan to southern Europe, where they settled in Nice. My grandmother was bored as hell in Nice, so she moved to Paris and met five other students who had the idea of traveling the world to spread peace after the war. It must have sounded crazy to her parents in 1948, because my grandmother was just in her early twenties.

But my great-grandparents were surprisingly forgiving and supportive. They said, "Okay, do it. We will give you our blessing." So my grandmother embarked on her journey around the world. In 1954 she published a wonderful book about her adventures, *Le Tour du monde avec cinq dollars* (Around the world on five dollars).

She eventually traveled to Calcutta and, after giving a lecture at the

University of Calcutta, attended by Sunil Janah, ended up staying on the roof of 57 Rashbehari for several weeks. My grandfather, Sunil's brother, fell in love with her. After she left India, he chased her to Paris. They both enrolled in the Sorbonne—my grandfather got a degree in ceramic arts. They moved back to Calcutta and opened the first fine-art ceramics studio in India.

My mother grew up in this world of intellectuals and artists—a really fascinating group of people. On the flip side, there was not a lot of stability; her parents weren't home very often. My mom grew up with lots of issues around that. At eighteen, she left home and studied in Bombay, where she met my father. He grew up in the south of India in a Christian family.

In 1978 they came to the United States, where they moved to—of all places—Buffalo, New York. It was really tough for two tropical people to arrive in a place with eight-foot-high snowdrifts. It was particularly hard on my mother. She wasn't working at the time—even though she had a degree in English, the best job she could get was slicing onions at Wendy's. They didn't have any money. I was born four years later, in 1982. I have a younger brother who is now studying at Stanford. Eventually, my family moved to Southern California.

Life Is a Birth Lottery

My father always sensitized me to issues of poverty. He subscribed to the *New Internationalist* calendar, which has beautiful photographs of people from developing countries, accompanied by statistics on poverty and income inequality. He taught us kids about inequity and that we had a duty to do something about it as we got older. My dad believes that all people have the right to dignity and should be treated equally. I learned so much from him about helping people. When Samasource received the Innovation Award from Secretary of State Hillary Clinton my father introduced himself as "Leila's dad." It was pretty cute.

When I was in middle school, a friend's grandmother recruited me to the local chapter of the American Civil Liberties Union. Some feisty retired people were helping students from Inglewood High School to get an Advanced Placement course at their school—the kind of educational advantage that is often available mainly to students in affluent school

districts. This was my first exposure to social justice issues and to the systemic inequalities that we've baked into our educational and economic systems. It was a real eye-opener for me.

Later I attended a fascinating public magnet high school, the California Academy of Math and Science. I went there because I was really interested in marine biology. There were only 120 students in my class, but they included people from every socioeconomic background. I'd always felt like the nerdy Indian girl, so being in a place where nobody had the advantages of money and mainstream American culture going for them but everyone was smart and motivated was just really exciting. There was also the sense that, for me as a woman, the sky was the limit. I got involved in international issues, starting a campus chapter of Amnesty International.

My parents didn't have much money, so I applied for literally every college scholarship that my guidance counselor had information about. My junior year I won a scholarship from the Lorillard Tobacco Company for $10,000. It felt kind of funny taking their money and putting it toward a fancy Ivy League education.

At the same time, I was growing more and more discontented with life in suburban L.A.: I was having issues with my parents and my peers; I had never seen a developing country; I wanted adventure. So in 2000 I found a program through the American Field Service that would enable me to work as a teacher with blind students in Ghana. I asked the scholarship committee if I could use the money to go to Ghana, and they agreed.

So off I went. I didn't know anything about teaching, I didn't know Braille, I had no lesson plans. Most important, I had never experienced anything like the poverty I saw there. Upon arrival, I could feel the intense suffering caused by poverty by seeing how people lived and dressed and what they had to do every day just to survive. It helped me understand how poverty oppresses people. Four billion people around the world have to live with that oppression every day. What shocked me most was seeing that these young people were equally capable as anyone else I'd ever met— they had just been born in the wrong place. Life really is a birth lottery.

I had one partially sighted student named Femi Abbas, who was from Nigeria. He was brilliant. He would listen to the Voice of America and BBC radio, absorbing everything like a sponge. I developed a close bond with this young kid, who had grown up on less than a dollar a day.

Over those six months I became more and more aware of the brain-power and talent at the bottom of the pyramid. There are people like Femi throughout the developing world. If only we could find a way to provide them with the same opportunities we have had, we could right a terrible wrong. I left Africa with a sense of urgency to do something about poverty.

The Making of a Social Entrepreneur

Back in America, at Harvard, I experienced reverse culture shock. I was incredibly depressed to find myself in the world of the elite boarding school crowd. So I did a special major in international development economics and figured out a way to spend every minute I wasn't in class in the field. I went to Senegal, India, and Brazil, and spent a summer in Rwanda.

I worked at Ashoka and the World Bank. I discovered that big institutions had a flawed model for ending poverty, because they really don't understand their customers—the extremely marginalized. In the world of economic development, there isn't the same level of innovation we have in Silicon Valley. I know CEOs who are billionaires who spend all their days talking to customers, trying to understand how they feel about their products. That kind of customer-centeredness is what leads to powerful new ideas. The development world lacks this focus.

So I decided to explore alternatives. I read Muhammad Yunus's first book, *Banker to the Poor*, which describes how he applied business principles to alleviating poverty. I decided that learning about business would probably be the best way I could help. In 2005 I joined Katzenbach Partners (now Booz & Company) in New York and was immediately sent to India to consult with a huge Indian outsourcing company.

One of the men working in the call center was from Dharavi—South Asia's largest and worst slum, where *Slumdog Millionaire* was filmed. The idea that this guy picking up phones to handle customers for British Airways—and speaking with an English accent—came from Dharavi was such a profound "Aha!" moment for me. It really started the wheels turning about what eventually became Samasource.

I realized we could create a pipeline between people like Femi Abbas and companies by using the Internet to provide them with livelihoods. After two years of hammering out various ideas and writing up a business plan, I quit my firm to get Samasource off the ground. *Sama* means "same" in Sanskrit, so the organization's name refers to leveling the playing field. It's a powerful word. It's not about equalizing income, it's about equalizing opportunity. I really believe in the marketplace and in the concept of individual agency.

"Grameen Bank has given me an unshakable faith in the creativity of human beings. This has led me to believe that human beings are not born to suffer the misery of hunger and poverty. To me, poor people are like bonsai trees. When you plant the best seed of the tallest tree in a flowerpot, you get a replica of the tallest tree, only inches tall. There is nothing wrong with the seed you planted, it's only the soil-base that is too inadequate. Poor people are bonsai people. There is nothing wrong in their seeds. Simply, society never gave them the base to grow on. All it needs to get the poor people out of poverty is for us to create an enabling environment for them. Once the poor can unleash their energy and creativity, poverty will disappear very quickly."

—From the 2006 Nobel Peace Prize lecture by Muhammad Yunus, founder of Grameen Bank

I also had the idea of working with the moral philosopher Dr. Thomas Pogge, whose book *World Poverty and Human Rights* I'd read as an undergrad. Pogge argues that we have a positive moral duty to do something about poverty—to help the four billion people who live on the equivalent of three dollars a day. I was living in New York at the time, and I wondered what it would feel like to stand outside with three dollars in my pocket and try to survive for a day. It would be terrible. So I got in touch with Dr. Pogge, who was then a professor of political philosophy at Columbia University, and helped him launch a not-for-profit organization called Incentives for Global Health.

In 2008 I ended up winning a business plan competition for my entry, "Market for Change." I had this idea that we could create a fair-trade label for services. I changed the name of the company from Market for Change to Samasource. I won twenty thousand euros and put all my eggs in the Samasource basket. I moved to Palo Alto and threw myself into my work.

The Audacity to Believe

For many people in the developing world, especially women, the sewing machine has been a lifeline out of poverty, because it can be used to

create goods for the marketplace. Now we are living in the digital age, so when a friend of mine describes the laptop as the "new sewing machine," I completely agree. It's basically the tool that an individual needs to become a producer in the new economy.

This is the idea behind Samasource. If we can find places where there's even the most basic computing infrastructure, we can turn them into microwork factories. We have experimented with a program in Dadaab, Kenya, one of the largest refugee camps in the world—a tragic place where more than 300,000 people live on less than a dollar a day. We also worked with a center in northern India to provide work to Tibetan refugees, and we work in Pakistan and Haiti.

The head of a large mobile company in Kenya told me that in two years, everyone in the country will be online. This is true across the developing world. We're having a huge amount of success. We are able to use the talent and human resources in places like Kenya by employing young people to do jobs like digitizing books for the blind. It's a throwback to my work with Femi!

We continue to innovate. Our biggest challenge is to build a great organization with the best people. We now have a small office in Nairobi and a functioning SamaLab—a small space devoted to testing the innovative uses of the microwork model in different field conditions. We recently experimented with the idea of using local Wi-Fi so workers could have access to work while remaining at home. This would cut down on commuting time for people who have families and for whom transportation is expensive. We are still developing this idea after launching a pilot program to test it in Kibera, an informal settlement in Nairobi.

We now are able to collect a lot more data about our workers and our methods; we discovered that some of our recruiting partners were sending us "higher-income" people who earned in the range of five dollars a day with previous work experience versus the three-dollars-a-day range mentioned on our website. These sorts of issues are hard to deal with because they require us to make judgments that seem a bit ridiculous from an office in San Francisco. Who is to say that three dollars a day is poor but five dollars a day is not? Both seem poor to me. But one of the goals we have as an organization is to dramatically move people out of poverty, and to do that effectively, we have to draw the line somewhere.

I think that throughout history there's been this pattern of resistance to change, and change-makers have to have thick skin about that. But we have shown it can work. It is important to start with an audacious goal.

One of my favorite places in San Francisco is the Martin Luther King, Jr., Memorial in Yerba Buena Gardens. Etched in stone there is a quote from his Nobel Peace Prize acceptance speech: "I have the audacity to believe that people everywhere can have three meals a day for their bodies, education and culture for their minds, and dignity, quality and freedom for their spirit." Today we're trying to help turn his audacious vision into reality. "

TO LEARN MORE ABOUT SAMASOURCE
please visit:

>Samasource
www.samasource.org
2017 Mission Street (Suite 301)
San Francisco, CA 94110

OTHER ORGANIZATIONS SUPPORTING SOCIAL
ENTREPRENEURSHIP:

>Acumen Fund
www.acumenfund.org
76 Ninth Avenue (Suite 315)
New York, NY 10011

>Ashoka: Innovators for the Public
www.ashoka.org
1700 North Moore Street
Arlington, VA 22209

>Echoing Green
www.echoinggreen.org
494 Eighth Avenue (2nd Floor)
New York, NY 10001

>Schwab Foundation for Social Entrepreneurship
www.schwabfound.org
91–93 Route de la Capite
CH–1223 Cologny/Geneva
Switzerland

>Skoll Foundation
www.skollfoundation.org
250 University Avenue (Suite 200)
Palo Alto, CA 94301

MASTER
OF MY FATE

the
Diahann Billings-Burford
story

CHIEF SERVICE OFFICER, NEW YORK CITY

ONE OF THE FIRST BOARDS I SERVED ON WAS PREP FOR PREP, which helps students of color compete at the highest levels in high school and college. Gary Simons, Prep for Prep's visionary founder, asked me to teach a summer course on William Ernest Henley's poem *Invictus* with Diahann Billings-Burford, an extraordinary graduate of Prep for Prep who was then attending Yale University. I was immediately taken by her determination and generous spirit.

In many ways Diahann's story captures the essence of what this book is about—following one's inner voice and passion, defying the expectations of others.

Today Diahann is leading a groundbreaking volunteer program in New York City. When I think of Diahann's journey, I hear echoes of the closing lines of *Invictus*:

> *I am the master of my fate:*
> *I am the captain of my soul.*

DIAHANN IS THE CHIEF SERVICE OFFICER OF NEW YORK CITY and leads NYC Service. In 2009 Mayor Michael Bloomberg established NYC Service, "to let loose an army of volunteers who will help tackle our biggest challenges." New York City is one of the largest cities in the world, with a population of over eight million. It is fast paced, vibrant, a true melting pot of people from around the world, and bursting with energy. It is a magnet for artists, innovators, dreamers, and the ambitious. It is a city where thinking big is business as usual.

The city's five boroughs—Manhattan, Brooklyn, Queens, the Bronx, and Staten Island—are home to some of America's wealthiest families and some of its poorest. Mobilizing the vast volunteer human resources of New York to serve the many hundreds of thousands of families in need of food, medicine, and housing, to tutor the city's public school children, and to make life safer and more civil, is more than a good idea: It is a way to ensure the city's physical and social health.

Diahann explains her mission this way:

> We are tasked with engaging more New Yorkers in strategic service and building service as a part of what it means to be a citizen of New York City. We oversee thirty-eight initiatives, targeting areas where we know we want to measure the impact that volunteers can have on meeting a pressing need. We have initiatives in six impact areas: strengthening our communities, helping our neighbors in need, education, the environment, health, and emergency preparedness.
>
> Our slogan is, we ask people to use their BLANK for good. The tagline means that everybody has something to offer. We believe that we will be able to make a culture shift, where everybody in New York understands that they have something to offer, no matter who they are.

Diahann's journey to a life of service began with her own journey as a young woman dealing with conflicting expectations and discovering the power of education.

Service Is a Natural Human Drive

"My father was a minister and an entrepreneur. My mom was an administrative assistant. I have five siblings. When I was four and wasn't quite old enough to go to kindergarten,

I lived with my grandparents for a year, because my mom and dad were both working. My mother always had incredibly high expectations of me.

She got me into an excellent public school in Brooklyn Heights. She knew that getting me into the right place would make a big difference in my life. She would bring the *New York Times* home from work and say, "Let's go. Let's see what you can read."

There were a lot of drugs in my neighborhood. The film *Notorious* told the story about the Notorious B.I.G., who sold drugs three blocks from my house. The expectation to use drugs was just around me, but I had very different expectations coming from my family. Navigating these different expectations was sometimes a challenge.

Many of my friends were early moms. Clearly, most of them are not having the career options I'm having, but I'm proud of the lives they've built for themselves and the successes they have made of their lives. In retrospect, if there's one experience in my life that changed my trajectory, it was Prep for Prep. Gary Simons saw my potential, and I will always be in debt to him for that.

I was planning to be a lawyer, but education always had a pull on me, so I made the decision at Yale that I would teach. I majored in psychology and teacher preparation. In college I had been an advisor for Prep for Prep and taught our course on *Invictus* for two summers. I was also a college counselor for Prep for Prep.

I was introduced to the concept of national service right before my senior year at Yale. I applied to be a White House intern in the Clinton administration and was placed in the office of National Service. I was pretty excited, because I was going to be in the White House. It was just a wonderful time.

Still, I had a lot to learn about national service. I wondered why people were motivated to give so much of themselves for little or no compensation. This was another turning point in my life, because I saw how powerful service can be in people's lives. People volunteer all their lives, but they just don't call it volunteerism. I realized that service was a natural human drive.

I began to think about service differently during my internship at the

White House. It made me more reflective about some of the opportunities I had been given. I came to appreciate Gary Simons more, because of the decisions and sacrifices he made for others.

After graduating from Yale in 1994, I taught at Kingswood Oxford School in West Hartford, Connecticut, for a year. After Kingswood, I got married. My husband and I moved to New York, and I entered Columbia Law School, graduating in 2002. I loved law school. It was also a personally challenging time for me. I had my son Rodney, who is deaf. I had my daughter during my third year, and I lost my mom while I was in law school. Fortunately, I have a wonderful husband—he was doing the work so I could go to school.

I began my legal career at Simpson Thacher & Bartlett, which is one of the greatest and largest law firms in the city. I was fortunate to work with Conrad Harper, one of the first African American partners in the city. Corporate law, however, was not a wonderful choice for me. I was making six figures and I enjoyed my time at Simpson but, quite honestly, I felt that in some ways I was moving by rote, not connected to my feelings and desires. I could see on the faces of my peers that this was where they wanted to be, and I didn't have that.

I returned to Prep for Prep to head up our Leadership Development Opportunities department. This was something I was meant to do. I was working for a bit more than half of my pay, but it was the right move. I felt like I was on the right seat on the bus. At first, my father and sister absolutely thought I'd lost my mind for giving up such a lucrative job, but in the end they were both incredibly supportive.

While I was at Yale I had met Dacia Toll, who was then attending Yale Law School, who started Amistad Academy, a charter school in New Haven. New York City schools chancellor Joel Klein asked her if she could replicate these schools in New York. Shortly thereafter, Dacia launched Achievement First in New York, and I joined her team as director of community and governmental affairs.

If I had to pick one mission that really speaks to me, it's educational equality. People use the slogan, "Education equals freedom." It's more than a slogan—it's my reality. Without education you don't have options. I believe that all children should be able to get a great education in public school.

That's what Achievement First is about. I am incredibly proud that I helped open four college preparatory public charter schools in central Brooklyn. Even though I no longer work at Achievement First, I sat on the board for Achievement First East New York Charter School for five years, and it means so much to me that the school is doing well.

I left Achievement First to become the deputy executive director for external affairs for City Year New York. It's a nonprofit organization that sends young tutors, mentors, and other volunteers into New York neighborhoods where their work is desperately needed.

I had a great time at City Year—those seventeen-through-twenty-four-year-olds helped me see more and more the untapped potential of national service. At City Year, I developed this belief in national service and what it could do for our country. I also began to see service as a solution to educational inequalities. But we don't have to stop there: Service can be the solution to public health concerns, environmental problems, and any other challenges that we face.

When I shifted from the for-profit to the not-for-profit world, I definitely gave up money, but money is about the only thing I gave up. I think that in every other arena, I gained. Money's important, but making a difference is more important than money.

It has been a real process and a real journey to get where I am right now. My role is to ensure that service is part of our culture.

In my current role as chief service officer, I get to lead such great initiatives as Flu Fighters. During the flu season we put out a call to action, asking New Yorkers to play one of three roles: community outreach, work at one of our vaccination clinics during the weekend, or bring people to public clinics during the flu season. We had almost 1,400 New Yorkers sign up, and we were able to give out more than 166,000 vaccinations. There are so many exciting programs for volunteers; very recently the mayor launched the Young Men's Initiative to address disparities between African American and Latino men and their peers, and our office has been tasked with examining the mentoring landscape in the city to identify best practices and build organizations' capacity to engage more New Yorkers as mentors.

Or take Cool Roofs as an example of an innovative environmental program. A NASA study released in March 2012 reported that on the hottest day during the summer of 2011, a white roof covering in New York was 42 degrees cooler than a traditional black roof. The goal of Cool Roofs is to coat roofs in New York City white to decrease our carbon footprint. It is our way of engaging citizens to help us reach our goal to reduce NYC's carbon footprint 15 percent by 2030. Cool Roofs has now coated more than 2.5 million square feet of New York City rooftop, and it is making a big difference in reducing the city's carbon footprint. Cool Roofs shows that when the private sector, the public sector, and the not-for-profit world work together, they can make things happen.

On the Journey

I wrote on my Facebook page the other day, "I absolutely love my job." We are facing some significant challenges, but it's our job as citizens to overcome them. My position allows me to focus on individual action, figure out how to bring it to scale, and make an impact on our city. In the end, it all hinges on an individual's decision to use his or her resources, time, and talent to help others.

Our biggest success has been changing the culture of service in city government. We have worked hard to encourage city agencies to think about how volunteers could expand their ability to impact New Yorkers' lives. Democracy can't exist without volunteerism and service.

But even with all the hard work, we still have to make some significant changes both in this country and globally. The disparity between the haves and have-nots is stark, and social mobility is frighteningly limited. I believe where civic engagement is vibrant, and when citizens are truly invested in their communities, they are better able to understand the complexity of our most pressing challenges. Invested citizens work for solutions.

I definitely feel as if I'm on my journey. I believe that everyone has a passion and a purpose. I don't think anything is wrong if a person's passion and purpose is making money. In fact, my ideas only work if some generous members of our society embrace that passion.

Before I finish this journey, wherever it takes me, I want people to be able to say the world is a better place because I was part of it. I want my legacy to be that I made a difference. **"**

TO LEARN MORE ABOUT NYC SERVICE
please visit:

>NYC Service
www.nycservice.org
c/o The Mayor's Office
City Hall
New York, NY 10007

OTHER ORGANIZATIONS OFFERING OPPORTU-
NITIES FOR VOLUNTEERING:

>AmeriCorps
www.nationalservice.gov
1201 New York Avenue NW
Washington, DC 20505

>Corporation for National and Community Service
www.nationalservice.org
1201 New York Avenue NW
Washington, DC 20525

>VolunteerMatch
www.volunteermatch.org
717 California Street (2nd Floor)
San Francisco, CA 94108

>Youth Service America
www.ysa.org
1101 15th Street NW (Suite 200)
Washington, DC 20005

MY DREAM IS MY DESTINY
the
Maria Pacheco
story

GENERAL MANAGER AND CO-OWNER, KIEJ DE LOS BOSQUES

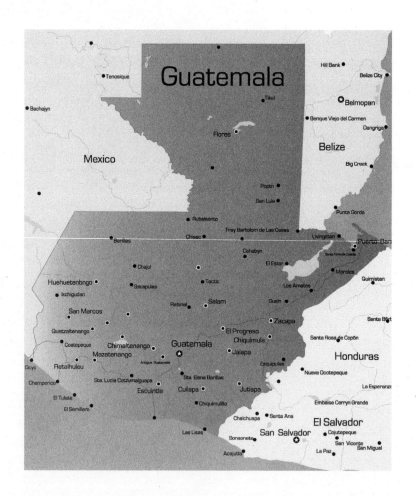

MARIA PACHECO IS STILL HAUNTED by the experience that defined her destiny. She was sixteen, working among the rural people of her country, Guatemala, and charged with the terrible task of handing mothers their own babies to bury, the tiniest victims of unforgiving poverty.

In that moment, Maria's passionate commitment to easing the plight of her people was born, along with a profound connection to Guatemala's rich cultural past and its land. Her deeply compelling story reminds us that we are all connected to the earth and to its people.

THE LARGEST COUNTRY IN CENTRAL AMERICA, Guatemala has a history of political turmoil. In 1996 peace accords were signed, ending thirty-six years of a bloody civil war in which 200,000 men, women, and children lost their lives and one million became refugees. Guatemala is also a very poor country; extreme poverty is common among the indigenous people. The country has one of the highest malnutrition rates in the world. It is also a very young country—38 percent of the population is under fourteen, and the median age is twenty.

Born in 1964, Maria has seen firsthand what war does. To cope with the destruction she saw around her, she turned to the warm abundance of nature and became an organic farmer. After working in the mountains of eastern Guatemala for nearly ten years, in 2004 Maria founded Kiej de los Bosques (Friends of the Trees), where she is general manager and co-owner. Its purpose is first to incubate businesses, starting them from a small seed and nurturing them into sustainable livelihoods, then to strengthen rural economic initiatives, design and develop new products, and provide access to markets.

In 2006 Maria and her partners established the Wakami Value Chain with the mission of "seeing the beauty in the world now!" The business model of Wakami is to create a network of rural communities where the fashion products of local women can be sold through an international export chain.

Today, Wakami is exporting fashion accessories to more than fifteen countries, including Europe, the United States, Canada, Mexico, Panama, and the Dominican Republic. Wakami products are sold by such outlets as Club Monaco, Brandy Melville, Ralph Lauren, and Natura. Maria believes that a few simple acts of entrepreneurship can create prosperity chains that can lift the very poor out of poverty. Like an ancient Mayan fable full of mysteries and surprises, Maria's life work evolved in partnership with the people she loves and serves.

Maria has been a consultant with the United Nations Foundation, is a Fulbright Scholar, and holds a master's degree in agriculture from Cornell University. She is married and the mother of three children. She is very active in promoting women's rights through Vital Voices and other international organizations. Several years ago, Maria wrote *Wakami's Gate*, a book telling the story of her life.

Healing a War-Torn World

"When I was twelve, my dad brought our family to the U.S. so he could study medicine. We lived in Kansas. When you're away from your country you can see it better. I realized that poverty was not normal. Four years later I came back to a Guatemala that was being torn apart by a civil war.

My family values are solidarity and sensibility. My dad is so very sensitive; it's almost like the world hurts him too much. My mom taught me the incubation business. She would work with the women. She got them sewing and started a sewing co-op that would export things. I entered the world through this kind of social point of view.

My mother and father started a clinic for the people who were running away from the war in the rural areas. My dad would see them as patients. You could really see the pain of the people. That was one thing that marked me. The other one is my brother, who is a Jesuit priest. Jesuits in Central America were really involved in trying to stop the killing. I was close friends with Jesuits that were writing about what was happening with the war, like Ricardo Falla. I said to myself, "I don't want to be part of this war."

When I was eighteen, I went to work for a refugee camp in the highlands. My job was to take sick kids from the refugee camp to the hospital. On the way to the hospital many kids would die. We would put them in a blanket and give them to their moms. The mom would walk to the village with her dead child, while we were trying to save the rest.

I think that moment of seeing a mother with a dead child was something that touched my heart. It made me say, either I get into a bubble and avoid seeing the world because it is too painful, or else I would do something about it. I couldn't feel okay when I knew what was happening to my country. I hated that I was part of a society where villages were being destroyed, where women were being raped, and where men were being killed.

I can feel people. I can feel things that come from them, and I wanted to help people.

During that time, I encountered the death of a little baby just because there was an IV solution missing. Ten dollars could have saved that kid. My city friends didn't have access to all this information, so they were like, "Oh Maria, she's a Communist, she's a leftist." And I'm like, "You guys, this is not about left and right. It's just about putting yourself with other people who are suffering. We have to do something."

One day I was writing my biology thesis, when I closed my eyes and had a dream. I envisioned a world that I would love to work in. My dream is my destiny. I shared it with my cousin and best friend, Queta. At that time Queta was helping me put everything into computers (I've never been too tech-wise). Queta wrote the dream on the computer: "I dream of a world in which the sound of the wind against the trees, the songs of birds from their nests, the jump of a lizard from one twig to another, the footsteps of a tiger in the soil, the breeze of spring in the home, and peace between brothers and sisters be everyday events."

Ten years later, Queta became my partner and a very important person in what we are doing. Living in a place like Guatemala without the dream, bitterness would have been something, because things are tough.

I remember we once gathered around a clandestine cemetery where three mothers had died, and for the first time people started talking about the war. Some guy said, "I want to kill somebody. I saw my dad being killed. I have so much hatred in me." So we dressed a little girl in white, and everybody in the community who felt hatred put their hands with a little earth on that little girl. And it came out that they had so much hatred and pain that they couldn't see the good opportunities, because they were living in the pain of the past. But slowly that changed. It's about transforming pain into hope, because that's what Guatemala really needs.

The people I worked with would say, "Maria, we need markets. If you find markets for us, we can do the rest." But finding markets really meant, "Go back to where you came from, because that's where people can buy things."

In the beginning I was teaching organic farming, because I decided that if I can't change the world, I can create my own, so I started organic farming. One of the farmers came to me and said, "Maria, I have the dream of planting trees." So in 1993 we started planting trees. The trees grew, and we had a sawmill, and then carpentry, and together with a friend, we developed a beautiful story and a brand they were selling.

Now they have their own company and they are still planting trees.

This place is called Sacala Las Lomas. The war had just finished, and an earthquake had hit their village really hard. I told my friend Patricio, "I don't have any money but I can work together with you guys." So he got ten friends, and we started planting three hundred trees each year. Now it's eight hundred people from eight communities planting trees.

We decided to found our own company, because we started realizing through markets you could transform the world and create the world you wanted. Kiej de los Bosques is a company with three values: valuing ancestral traditions, recovering ecological systems, and bringing new people into prosperity chains. We also decided to create the brand Wakami, which means "the world is already great," as a way of distributing products from rural communities to the world.

So now we have what we call an inclusive business system. Through the NGO Communities of the Earth, we're incubating eighteen rural companies. We are designing the Wakami products and exporting to the world. We are exclusive importers in each region of the world. They are key to promoting the brand and generating sales. So now it's one company and one NGO called the SAQIL Group, which means "The earth is bright when the sun shines."

The Power of Kiej

For me the Mayan people are very special. I met a person who explained to me that, according to the Mayan calendar, I was born with a mission. There are twenty days in a Mayan calendar. One of those days is Kiej. That day represents the energy which brings balance between nature and human beings. Kiej has a bit of the energy of the four cardinals: north, east, west, and south. We're supposed to be the sign that brings harmony into things.

The Mayan calendar tells you where you've come from and where you're going. My Mayan calendar tells me I come from community. Anything I do that has to do with community just goes

really well. It's like I need community to feel alive. So for me it's like, wow, those Mayans are really wise!

I feel the Mayan calendar is really about knowing how energy flows—how it flows in people, in nature, and in the universe. If you can link to that, it is beautiful and an invitation. It puts me in touch with Guatemala. I feel like something's missing when I'm not in touch with Guatemala. I think it has to do with the Mayans, who are so linked to the earth—a very simple life that reminds you of the beauty of life.

One of my favorite communities is Jocotán in the mountainous eastern part of Guatemala. The Chorti Indians live there. I like going into those communities, because your mind goes to quietness and to appreciating those mountains, those people, those houses—everything so earthy. The little houses are made of palm leaves and adobe, and the people wear very bright dresses. They weave the *petate* [dried palm leaves], which we transform into products. Mayans say that weaving *petate* is weaving time and space.

It's a very dry ecosystem, and there was a famine there. Kids were dying of hunger. But once you are able to make them part of a supply chain, their lives really start prospering. For me it's almost like Shambhala, that ideal place where everything flows peacefully.

Expanding the Dream

Eight years ago someone from Holland came and said, "We love what you do. We want to fund you." Amazed, I said, "You want to fund my dream?" So we started a trust fund and started working with the community. The changes you can see are wonderful.

Like Doña Santa. She invited me to her house. She had a kid lying on the floor, and I said to her, "Your kid is going to die." And she said, "I have three dollars in my pocket. With those I can try to save this kid or try to feed the other seven for the rest of the month." I said, "How can I help you?" And

she said, "If you can sell what we produce, the rest we can do." Those words became our command.

So the women started producing, and we linked these rural communities to global companies. We became a bridge and incubator. Famine has stopped in the communities. Mothers with income pushed the local mayor to build a junior high school and two years ago a high school. So now we're having kids going to college in a community where you had just two years of schooling before.

Doña Santa first bought one cow and then two, and now she has land. Of three hundred women in the community, 260 have savings accounts. Two months ago they opened a savings and loan co-op. When these women that I work with get their first paycheck, you can see the light in their eyes. You see the community working. Change is happening. People start dreaming again. That's what I'm passionate about.

We have people who love going into the communities and teaching the women. We have technicians in the field that speak the local language and translate the incubation methodology, which we love, because it starts with people's dreams. My job now is just to keep dreaming and telling the story to other people.

The power of dreams is very strong, but the power of collective dreams is amazing. What for us was a dream is now a system that is able to bring new people into prosperity chains, transforming entire communities forever. Be your dream.

As we grow, we can generate thousands of jobs for Guatemalan women. We've started to create the concept of Wakami Villages, which are communities that have sustainable ways of living. We're going to plant trees, we're going to recycle trash, and we're going to do green gardens. Happily, I'm getting back into gardening again—I have to find an excuse!

My journey is changing as my role is changing. Now I inspire people and support a team of amazing women and men. If there is one thing I have learned, it is the power of teamwork. I have no words when I look back at how we started and see where we are now and the potential for growth—it is so beautiful to see it happening in front of your eyes. Value chains can transform everything.

Guatemala is facing some very tough challenges due to poverty and a violent drug war. But the newly elected government is giving people hope. Finding programs that work and strengthening institutions is key. Getting women involved is also essential. Women need to become involved at all levels of society.

I think my lesson is that you start small no matter what. Just make sure it's within the dream, and it will grow. We can transform everything through connection, through connection with ourselves and through connection with the earth. For me it's important just to feel the earth.

If you only see pain and don't have something positive to move forward to, it's really easy to get bitter and hard. But I think it's a totally different journey if you're really moving toward something beautiful. These energies are different. "

TO LEARN MORE ABOUT KIEJ DE
LOS BOSQUES
please visit:

>Kiej de los Bosques
www.kiejdelosbosques.com
www.wakami.net

Via 1, 1-67 Zona 4
Edificio Rodseguros, 4° Nivel
Guatemala Ciudad 01004
Guatemala

OTHER ORGANIZATIONS DEVELOPING RURAL
ECONOMIES IN CENTRAL AMERICA:

>Earthworks
www.earthworksaction.org
1612 K Street NW (Suite 808)
Washington, DC 20006

>Inter-American Development Bank
www.iadb.org
1300 New York Avenue NW
Washington, DC 20577

>The Nature Conservancy
www.nature.org
4245 North Fairfax Drive (Suite 100)
Arlington, VA 22203

>World Wide Opportunities
on Organic Farms
www.wwoof.org
430 Forest Avenue
Laguna Beach, CA 92651

I HOPE THEY HAVE
LOVE

the
Sara Horowitz
story

FOUNDER AND EXECUTIVE DIRECTOR, FREELANCERS UNION

MY HUSBAND, KEN, WOULD HAPPILY ADMIT he met his match in
Sara Horowitz. A MacArthur "genius" awardee with a deliciously
self-deprecating sense of humor, Sara captivated us from our first
introduction. With a twinkle in her eye, she engaged Ken in a lively
discussion about the pros and cons of the labor movement's impact on
America's economic growth.

Although she was open-minded and willing to consider Ken's proposal
that she turn her not-for-profit, now called Freelancers Union, into a for-
profit enterprise, she didn't succumb. In the end Ken, too, fell under her
spell—as so many others have. I sighed with relief.

FREELANCERS—INDEPENDENT WORKERS—make up 30 percent of the
American workforce. These "solopreneurs" work in film and television,
advertising, graphic design, health care, journalism, fashion, financial
services, and many more fields. Freelancers are an essential part of the
economy, yet generally they have no health insurance, no retirement plans,
no one to represent them, and few professional communities to join.
Freelancers are America's invisible workforce.

At least they *used* to be invisible. Over a decade ago, Sara Horowitz
decided to end this invisibility and the exploitation that goes with it. She
founded Freelancers Union, a federation of the unaffiliated, dedicated to
the guiding principles of mutual support and social entrepreneurship.

Sara sees Freelancers Union as the next step for unionism, the natural historic successor to craft and industrial unions. Freelancers represent a new kind of workforce, a group that has fallen out of the social safety net. The last time a similar social mismatch happened was in the 1920s and 1930s. In response, industrial workers formed the unions that played a major role in catalyzing Franklin D. Roosevelt's New Deal.

Sara is working to bring people together, to help them solve the problems of their day-to-day lives, such as health insurance and retirement security. Her larger goal is to build a social safety net for the next generation of workers. Freelancers Union has more than 180,000 members in all fifty states and continues to grow. In 2012, Freelancers was named as the sponsor for $340 million in federal loans to help start new nonprofit, member-driven health plans in Oregon, New York, and New Jersey. Recently, Freelancers Union opened up a practice in Brooklyn to provide primary health care to thousands of self-employed New Yorkers.

The Political Gene

"I always knew I was going to do something in the labor movement—in fact it never occurred to me that I would do something different. I've been working for unions since I was eighteen. My grandfather was vice president of the International Ladies' Garment Workers' Union, and my father was a labor lawyer. My grandmother lived in union housing, and we'd go to visit every Sunday. I'm a Brooklyn girl.

My parents talked about politics all the time. I'm an insomniac and so was my father. He had me when he was forty-five, and we'd sit up till one in the morning, talking politics. He would always say, "I just want to know who you're going to vote for, 'cause I know they're not going to win."

My father grew up in the Bronx and served in World War II. He wanted to avoid going to the front, so he read some books on meteorology and worked as a meteorologist during the war. His sense of social ethics was always driving him. One time, for example, when he was stationed in Texas, he was hitchhiking with a friend who was black. When a car stopped and the driver said, "I'll take you but not your friend," my father replied, "I'm staying with my friend."

So let me just say my mother and father are both dead. (This will be where I cry.) As a mother, I think a lot about what I learned from my own mother. The way she lived her life will always stay with me. I was raised to believe you have an obligation to serve a purpose higher than yourself. But my parents didn't believe in rules just for the sake of rules. You couldn't let yourself off the hook that easily.

My parents raised me to talk to everyone the same way, whether he or she is an elected official or someone who's cleaning a hotel room. They're all of the same worth. Once you start realizing that we're all God's children, you recognize that our obligation in life is to see ourselves as human beings.

I went to a Quaker school, where the belief in human dignity was reinforced. I remember calling a strike of all the girls on International Women's Day when I was in eighth grade. I didn't think anyone would listen to me, so I went up to my first class, and when I came down, the girls went on strike. That was wild.

I went to Stuyvesant High School, where I met my future husband, although we didn't date until after college. My husband's name is Peter Dante DeChiara, and he's Jewish. He grew up in Queens (don't hold it against him!). He's very tall and cute and quiet and tough. I've been trying to boss him around for twenty-three years, and I've been unsuccessful. Peter is a very interesting person, a really good dad, and gives me a lot of strength. I hope I do the same for him. He's a lawyer for unions.

I have a sister, and she's a political person. Her daughter Natalie is like my daughter—she has the political gene. When Natalie was about ten, she was on a walking tour of the White House during the Bush administration, and she just started screaming, "I hate George Bush!" And I said, "Oh my God, she has the gene!"

My daughter was born January 27, which is Sam Gompers's birthday, the founder of the AFL [American Federation of Labor]. She puts things together about politics, race, and economics. I am sure that when other kids go home, they don't talk about the same things she does. She has the hard questions in her head, because she's trying to understand things, and I love that.

I went to the labor school at Cornell and then attended law school, after which I became a criminal defense lawyer with Legal Aid in New York.

I really loved it, although it was a hard job. I became the shop steward for the union and said to myself, "Enough already. I'm just going to stick with this. This is what I believe in and this is what I want to do."

I'm a good entrepreneur. It's funny—I come from a lefty family where there's no real love of the idea of entrepreneurialism, but I love the idea of putting things together. I have a deep-seated need to make sure I'm building something. Unionism and entrepreneurialism aren't mutually exclusive. Americans need to know the vital role unions have played in every social movement in our history. Supporting unions means recognizing their great contribution, but it also means recognizing the need for unions to evolve to meet the needs of future generations.

After all, unions were the first organizations to build health clinics and affordable housing. My hero is Sidney Hillman, who was the head of the Amalgamated Clothing Workers union. He put together the first model of unemployment insurance. The same model was later adopted by the Roosevelt administration.

Weaving a New Social Safety Net

In the spirit of bringing people together, I started to find out what were the biggest problems in people's lives. At the time (the mid-1990s) the biggest problem was health insurance, especially for people who were self-employed. As part of this work, I ended up starting Freelancers Union with the goal of grouping people together to purchase health insurance and other vitally needed services.

Freelancers Union is the quarterback. We are a not-for-profit organization but we have created a for-profit insurance company that we own, so there are no private shareholders. We make sure that any return is reinvested into research and development as well as lower insurance premiums. We're setting up a credit union now. Just as we build on the work of others, we hope people will build from us.

Like almost any social movement, our first job was to say, "We're here. We need to be counted. These are our needs." The union enables people to come together regularly, whether it's for educational groups, to meet with elected officials, to network, or just to have holiday parties. We give freelancers a sense of camaraderie, which in turn generates pride.

Our logo is a picture of bees buzzing around a hive. This represents people who are doing their work independently but coming together in a hive to build an entire society—just as freelancers do the work of the country.

Today the union has nearly two hundred thousand members nationally. Our biggest states are California, New York, and New Jersey—we represent about ninety thousand people in New York alone. We're becoming one of the largest unions in the country, especially in the private sector.

Freelancers can be the pioneers of change. They can be the ones to change capitalism from a private-equity, quick-moving system exploiting a disposable workforce into a system that recognizes and rewards workers, builders, and creators. We are seeing a broader path for this movement that involves a wider network of allies, partners, key influencers, members, and freelancers at large. Technology enables us to connect with stakeholders where they are—on networks of networks and platforms of platforms. The social web (Twitter, Facebook, Quora, FourSquare, etc.) presents exciting opportunities for expansion, connection, and engagement.

Before Freelancers Union was founded, insurance companies would just say to the self-employed, "Oh, you're basically just an individual; go out there and buy your own insurance." We said, "Wait a minute! We have got to think beyond this fee-for-service model, where doctors get paid by body part." So we grouped people together to purchase health insurance and disability and life insurance and to advocate for the things they need.

We're looking at new ways to get care. For example, we're partnering with community groups to create medical homes, where as soon as you come in you're assigned a doctor, a social worker, a nurse practitioner, and a nutritionist. You get the full view of your health needs, all your medical records are under one roof, and your care is integrated. The goal is to treat people as whole human beings, integrating nontraditional health care, nutrition, and acupuncture with the traditional care.

We also advocate for the next social safety net, something many freelancers have to create on their own. If they have a period of time where there is no work, there's no unemployment insurance; there's nothing for them. They are going to charity hospitals and living on other people's couches. Freelancers aren't the only ones for whom the system has stopped working. We are, in a very stark way, losing our middle class. Creating the next safety net is basic to our democracy.

I was recently in Portland, Oregon, and was so impressed with how many people have chosen to live in a simple, sustainable, and mutually

supportive way. This movement toward simplicity and community is building a new solidarity that makes me feel very hopeful about the future.

Overcoming Loneliness

What worries me so much is that we are becoming a society composed of a small group of rich people and a large group of everybody else. In the process we're becoming more and more isolated from each other. Many people feel they are profoundly alone and not connected anymore—I hope they have love. We expect our government to do something for us, but we could have power if we connected to other people.

After doing this for fifteen years, one of the joys for me has been watching the next generation of people I work with, who are social entrepreneurs in their own right and who know way more than me, dedicating their lives to building organizations themselves. When you're plugging into something greater than yourself, you're helping others, they're helping you, you're learning from them, they're learning from you—it's all a privilege.

I really feel like we're at the beginning of a different era. We can't wait for the future—it's already here. I often say to the young people I work with, "It's our obligation to figure things out, to come around a table and be kind and really focus together." So much of life is about love. If you are part of building something that builds up love, you're the luckiest person in the world. Don't judge what your contribution is; just find your contribution and find people that inspire you. Don't judge yourself and don't judge others. **"**

TO LEARN MORE ABOUT FREELANCERS UNION please visit:

>Freelancers Union
www.freelancersunion.org
20 Jay Street (Suite 700)
Brooklyn, NY 11201

OTHER ORGANIZATIONS REPRESENTING WORKERS IN THE NEW ECONOMY:

>American Society of Journalists and Authors
www.asja.org
1501 Broadway (Suite 403)
New York, NY 10036

>Freelance Cafe
http://freelancecafe.org

>National Association of Freelance Legal Professionals
www.naflp7.camp7.org
44-489 Town Center Way (Suite D436)
Palm Desert, CA 92260

>The Authors Guild
www.authorsguild.org
31 East 32nd Street (7th Floor)
New York, NY 10016

I HAD A PURPOSE

the
Vivian Nixon
story

EXECUTIVE DIRECTOR,
THE COLLEGE AND COMMUNITY FELLOWSHIP PROGRAM

College &
Community
Fellowship

VIVIAN NIXON SAYS HER DREAM of becoming a stage actress was crushed by her mother's hurtful words: "You are not beautiful. You will never be an actress." But today Vivian is a star in a very different role.

After falling in with a bad crowd and spending several years in prison, she emerged stronger, with a new dream—the dream of giving women just released from prison a second act through education and jobs.

Her amazing resilience in the face of personal setbacks gives hope to people of every age and circumstance that they, too, can make something of themselves and make a difference.

VIVIAN IS THE DIRECTOR OF THE COLLEGE AND COMMUNITY FELLOWSHIP (CCF), which was founded in 2000. Women who enroll in CCF's programs come from New York City, Long Island, and Westchester County. CCF provides formerly incarcerated women with academic counseling, college level tutoring and mentoring, and programs in career development, financial literacy, community building, leadership development, artistic expression, and public policy and advocacy. More than 70 percent of CCF students are recovering from addiction; 75 percent are mothers; 50 percent are survivors of domestic abuse; 85 percent are women of color. Women participating in CCF's program have a less than 2 percent recidivism rate, and 80 percent complete the program. More than 300 students have received tuition assistance and academic and financial counseling since CCF's founding. Participants have been awarded 35 associate degrees, 105 bachelor's degrees, 50 master's degrees, and 1 doctoral degree. One hundred percent report increased earnings postgraduation. Many have won prestigious academic awards and honors, and many volunteer as mentors and tutors.

Vivian was chosen to be an Ascend Fellow for the Aspen Institute in 2012 and plans to launch a women's health initiative in 2013 that will include developing a program that deals with the many issues children of incarcerated parents face. CCF is also collaborating with the Fortune Society's David Rothenberg Center for Public Policy on a project called Education from the Inside Out Coalition. The coalition works on improving public policies that limit access to higher education for people in prison or who have recently reentered society.

"That's Just Vivian"

"I had what some people might call an average start in life, growing up on Long Island with my parents. My mom worked for the telephone company for many years; she started right out of high school and became a phone operator when they were still wearing roller skates.

My dad was in the military, then worked for a while as a short-order cook, and ultimately ended up in the construction business, working in a plant that manufactured cement pipes. That's what he did until he was too sick to work because of the dust from the cement and all the other stuff that nobody cared about back then. He retired and passed away soon thereafter.

I always had these huge dreams of doing something big with my life. I felt I was called to be great in some way, although I didn't know in what way. I aspired to be a stage actress at one time and took a lot of theater courses. In high school I was in the chorus and joined theater groups.

But my parents never supported any of those notions. It was all nonsense to them and a sure way to fail. So as a result of not feeling supported in who I really was, I was a fairly depressed teenager. All I knew was that I wasn't happy. I didn't know it was clinical, and I didn't know there was help out there for me.

My parents certainly didn't recognize that a teenager who spends more time alone than with other people is not normal. They said, "That's just Vivian. That's just who she is." My depression got worse and worse over time.

They shipped me off to Oswego State University in upstate New York when I was eighteen with clear instructions that I should major in something that was going to lead to a productive career. I was supposed to major in political science and become a lawyer one day. But instead I majored in theater.

A pivotal point in my life came when I got my grades after my first year in college. I remember my mother opened the envelope from college; she saw I'd gotten outstanding grades in the theater courses but didn't do so well in the other courses. She was furious.

I'll never forget the words she used—they changed my life. She said, "You are not beautiful. You will never be an actress."

I don't really remember what happened after that. I know I didn't go back to school. I got a job at the phone company, and my life just became this black hole of depression and sadness. Everybody drinks and smokes pot in high school and college, but for me it became more and more of a lifestyle. In my twenties and early thirties I started using cocaine and went into a steep downward spiral.

In a way, I was leading a double life, because while I was miserable in my job, I was also doing the things my parents expected of me. We were very involved in the church, and I attended church every Sunday.

In the early 1980s a woman pastor came to the church. She was not only an ordained minister but a certified social worker and a psychotherapist. She was very different than the other ministers we'd had at the church. She did not come with a message of doom and gloom or fire and brimstone. It was more about healing, embracing who we are, and seeing the divine in each of us.

She recognized immediately that I had issues, including addiction problems and depression. She made sure I got treatment. Again, this was not supported by my family, particularly my mother, who did not understand what I needed and that getting help didn't mean I was "crazy."

But because of the pastor, my life began to change. I began to embrace who I was and tried to find ways to achieve the higher calling I always knew was in me. I began to study religion and spirituality and started a church group of other women who suffered similar problems. I felt useful. I stopped using drugs. I was moving in the right direction.

Back to a Place of Darkness

But then my past caught up with me. One day the Nassau County District Attorney's Office came knocking at my door about crimes I'd committed two and three years in the past—paper crimes, like forgery. They could still prosecute me and they did. It was a very difficult time, one that sent me back to that place of darkness I thought I had escaped from.

After a year's wait, I was sentenced to three and a half to seven years in prison. I was devastated. But I tried to make the best of a bad situation. I did not want my family to own it. I took total blame for it. In fact, once they shipped me up to Albion Correctional Facility, I forbade my family to make the eight-hour trip to visit me. For the three and a half years I was in prison, I didn't see my family.

Before I went to Albion, I went to Bedford as a transitional facility, where they had a college program. Within the first three days of being at Bedford, I registered for college. I felt hopeful for the first time. But a week and a half later, they shipped me off to Albion, which does not have a college program. So I went through another bout of depression.

At Albion I got involved with a group of women who met on a weekly basis in the prison chapel. They were really spiritually grounded. Some of the women had been in prison for ten or twenty years. I started to think, *Who am I to wallow in depression, when these women who have a plight much worse than mine have found a way to find some light and are able to help other women?*

So I started to look for ways to help other women. That is when I found the adult education GED [General Educational Development] program. I became a tutor. I sat with older women who could barely read their own names. It broke my heart.

It made me wonder, "How did we ever expect these women to have a chance?" Their illiteracy was just another problem on top of all the other problems they had to deal with, like domestic violence, the tragic loss of children and family, and poverty.

I began to devote my life to that GED tutoring program, helping as many women as possible get as far as they could with their education. In time it became much more than a job. I found myself spending time helping them with homework, helping them write letters, helping them to correspond with their lawyers, and helping them read and interpret the mail they received.

It became my life. I was not wasting my time. I had a purpose. I knew that the things that I wanted for myself would come eventually. But during that time my purpose was to be a light for these women who'd had nothing but darkness in their lives. Compared to the lives of these women, mine was privileged, and I had thrown that privilege away.

"I Want Your Job"

I began to think about what I would do when I left prison. I knew it wouldn't be anything that I had ever thought of before. But I knew it would be in service to these women.

Looking back, it seems serendipitous, but I think it was divine inter-vention, because about two or three weeks before I left prison, someone handed me a brochure for College and Community Fellowship. It was almost as if someone had invented a solution just for me. It seemed too good to be true. But it was quite true.

I had an interview with Benay Rubenstein, who was the first director of the program, which was founded by Barbara Martinsons. She asked me what I wanted to do. So I said to her, "I want your job." She laughed and said, "Well, you know, maybe you ought to consider majoring in human services administration." That's exactly what I did. After I got my degree, Benay was leaving the organization, and—just as I'd dreamed—I got her job. It was unbelievable.

At the time, CCF was in a transitional phase. The founder had given a great deal of money to start the organization, but not much planning had been devoted to figuring out how to sustain it. We were running out of money. We had about a year to start raising some real money. I don't know where the strength or the knowledge I needed came from, but somehow I got meetings with the heads of foundations and convinced them that help-ing women from prison earn college degrees is a worthy goal.

One of the things that hurt my mother the most was that while I was in prison and on parole I could not vote. That was the most important factor to her. I didn't really understand it. But last year, after my mother passed away,

I was cleaning out some of her things and found her original voter registration card. On the day she turned twenty-one she went down to the Board of Elections and registered to vote. It was really important to her—to be a participant in society and influence her own destiny and her children's destiny.

That's something I think education does for women. I've seen it happen. When our students graduate, they become engaged in our society in a way they had never been before. Education doesn't just help you get a better job; it makes you a better citizen. It's not a silver bullet for the problems of our society, but it will reduce crime a great deal.

The past few years have taught me that this work has the potential to have a broader impact than I dreamed possible. I've learned just how connected issues of crime, poverty, racism, classism, and sexism are to what many women go through and shape the way society views people who have broken the social contract. CCF and similar programs should be part of a larger education agenda that focuses not just on the success of individuals but on the success of the nation.

At CCF I can marry my zest for people, my belief in human wholeness and individual development, and my spirituality with my love of public speaking. For years, I've declined to tell the "gory details" of my journey. That's changing now, and I have begun taking notes in preparation for writing a memoir. If telling my story can help one person who is struggling with similar issues, then it is a story worth telling. It has all come together for me.

That's how I know this is the thing I was meant to do. **"**

TO LEARN MORE ABOUT THE COLLEGE
AND COMMUNITY FELLOWSHIP
please visit:

>College and Community Fellowship
www.collegeandcommunity.org
475 Riverside Drive (Suite 1626)
New York, NY 10115

OTHER ORGANIZATIONS ENABLING
DISADVANTAGED WOMEN TO ATTEND COLLEGE
AND GAIN EMPLOYMENT:

>Catalyst
www.catalyst.org
120 Wall Street (5th Floor)
New York, NY 10005

>Center for Employment Opportunities
www.ceoworks.org
32 Broadway (15th Floor)
New York, NY 10004

>Greenhope Services for Women
www.greenhope.org
435 East 119th Street (7th Floor)
New York, NY 10035

>The Correctional Association
of New York
www.correctionalassociation.org
2090 Adam Clayton Powell Blvd. (Suite 200)
New York, NY 10027

TO BE TRULY
HUMAN

the
Jacob Lief
story

PRESIDENT AND CO-FOUNDER, UBUNTU EDUCATION FUND

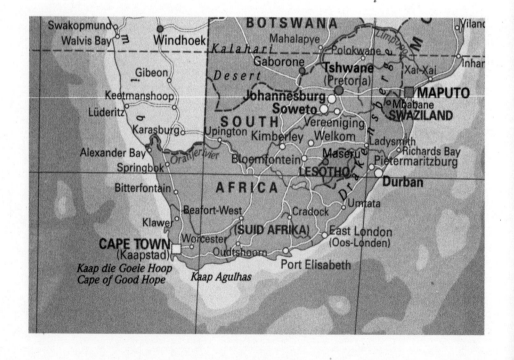

J ACOB LIEF STARTLES EVERYONE IN THE ROOM as he proudly announces the name of his brand-new baby son: Freedom—which leaves no doubt as to where his passion lies. Bursting with charm and charisma, Jacob is positively electrifying as he talks about building a comprehensive education/health program in a South African township over the past thirteen years, the Ubuntu Education Fund.

Beneath his casual and unassuming appearance, there is a fierce determination and a deep sense of fairness. His goal: to provide "his" South African children with the highest quality education and health care, the kind the most privileged parents in America demand—and get—for their own children.

THE HOME OF UBUNTU EDUCATION FUND (Ubuntu) is the Zwide township in Port Elizabeth, in the Eastern Cape province of South Africa. In 1997 Jacob happened to get off the train in Port Elizabeth, where he met Banks Gwaxula in a *shebeen,* or local bar. They formed a lasting friendship and together founded Ubuntu in 1999. Today Jacob is president of Ubuntu, providing life-saving HIV services and essential educational resources to over four thousand orphaned and vulnerable children and their families.

A recent study by McKinsey & Company found that 96 percent of

Ubuntu clients adhere to their HIV treatments, 94 percent are successful with their TB treatments, Ubuntu students excel in school and are well on their way to productive lives, and perhaps the most startling statistic of all—a one-dollar investment in an Ubuntu child results in nearly nine dollars in lifetime earnings for him or her.

Archbishop Desmond Tutu says this about the meaning of *Ubuntu:* "We Africans speak of ubuntu, the recognition of humanity in one another." This belief in a common human destiny is the heart and soul of Jacob's passion for justice. Ubuntu is more than a way to do business; it is a way to be.

"I Have Been Waiting Eighty-Five Years"

"I was born in New York City, but we moved to suburban New Jersey when I was a kid. My father worked for Goldman Sachs his whole life. He had this incredible, high-powered, sort of crazy, ridiculous work ethic. My mother was always helping others— my brother and I had to wake up at four in the morning to do the soup kitchens; we had to read to blind people—it was just how my mother was raised in Pennsylvania. Her sense of service is in my DNA.

My family moved to London when I was thirteen. My mother ran the Thames River soup kitchen. I remember we brought over eight Palestinian and eight Israeli kids to live with us. None of them had met each other before. That was like our family's peace resolution thing.

I was playing soccer in Hyde Park one day, when I saw a giant "Free Mandela" march. I knew nothing about South Africa. I asked someone what was going on, and they said, "We're distributing flyers." I started passing out flyers and volunteering right then. In 1994 I went to South Africa with a group of students to observe the elections.

There is a story I tell all the time, because it really changed my life. We were in Alexandra, which is a township made up of shacks and corrugated iron roofs. I met an older woman and we started talking. She told me she had stood in line five days to vote. When I said, "You waited in line five days just to vote!" she tapped me on the shoulder and said, "No, boy, I have been waiting eighty-five years."

I had never thought about freedom before. I went to good schools. I had all the opportunities. And here was a woman who had waited eighty-five years for the right to vote. Right then I said, "I want to become part of the new South Africa."

I started to research where I wanted to go to university. I discovered that Dr. Mary Frances Berry, a law professor at the University of Pennsylvania and a leader in the anti-apartheid movement, taught at Penn. I said to myself, "I'm going to Penn."

I enrolled in 1995, but because I was a freshman, I was ineligible for Dr. Berry's law and public policy classes. But I kept bugging and bugging her. Meanwhile, I was desperate to get back to South Africa and struggling with being at Penn. While it's an incredibly diverse campus, it's also incredibly segregated as well. If you're black, you're allowed to go into the Du Bois house; if you're conservative Jewish, you go into the Hillel house, and so on.

I spent the summer after my freshman year thinking about these issues. I went home to Maine for the summer, worked in my parents' restaurant, and found myself saying, "I'm not going back to Penn. I'm gonna work on a lobster boat." So I took five months off to work on a lobster boat called

"I first met Jacob Lief in January of 2006. He bounded into the lobby of my New York hotel, a young man with long, curly, blond hair, an infectious smile, and a palpable passion for South Africa and his organization, Ubuntu Education Fund. His energy took over the room. The first thing I asked him was: 'What is a white American like you doing in the townships?' He answered, in the unembellished, undaunted way that I now recognize as his trademark style, 'I'm trying to give the kids there the same kind of education you and I would give our own children.' "

—Archbishop Desmond Tutu, describing his first meeting with Jacob

Just a Plug In. It was beautiful. I was out on the water for twelve hours a day, thinking and thinking.

Finally, I said to myself, "My way back to South Africa is to get my degree." So I went back to school and started bugging Dr. Berry again. She finally let me into her class. Dr. Berry and I became good friends, and I convinced her to help me go back to South Africa. Soon thereafter, she arranged for me to leave school early.

Bonding with Banks

Meanwhile, I had found an organization to work for in Cape Town. But when I got there, it turned out to be a complete scam. I said to myself, "Shit, I can't go back to Dr. Berry. She's as tough as they come, and she'll kill me." So after one day at this organization, I got on a train out of Cape Town. On the train I met a guy and we started talking. Eventually, he said, "Why don't you get off in Port Elizabeth? We call it the Detroit of South Africa. Come have a drink with me."

So I made this huge decision, although I didn't know it at the time. I got off the train and went with him to a little *shebeen* in New Brighton township.

There had never been a white man in this tavern before. When I walked in, it was literally like a scene out of a movie, where the needle scratches and everyone looks up. This one guy said to me, "Come over here and let me talk to you." It was Banks. We hit it off instantly. He is named after Gordon Banks, the famous English soccer goalkeeper, and had grown up to be a goalkeeper himself. I was a goalkeeper too, so I loved him. We bonded.

I told Banks that the project I was supposed to be working on had turned into a disaster, and my professor in the States was going to kill me. He said, "Don't worry, you can come work in my school. The students are as poor as you'll find. You can stay with me." It never occurred to me he didn't live alone. It should have.

The minute we walked in the house, everyone started screaming. They thought I was the police. The legacy of apartheid is difficult to overcome. People sometimes couldn't look me in the eye because I am white. But everyone calmed down when Banks explained, "This is Jacob, and he's going to live with us."

Over the next five months I lived in this community. I didn't have a cell phone; I didn't have a car; I worked at schools that had no supplies. In my spare time I played on the local soccer team.

When I tried to figure out how life in this community could be improved, what I saw was European Union money and big nonprofits from Washington, D.C., coming in and distributing things like computers, cups of soup, and blankets. It was all nice work. But they would come in, do a few workshops, and then they'd be out, leaving behind all the problems.

Meanwhile, I continued working with Banks. He has an incredible will and the ability to mobilize people. That was the beginning of my understanding that bottom-up development is the way to make a lasting difference. About two weeks before I was due to take off, Banks woke me up at four in the morning. He

"For several years, the important work of dealing with the effects of HIV/AIDS became derailed by politics. Some wanted to argue about its causes, arguing over what remedies were most effective and how the epidemic might be staunched. Meanwhile, thousands of children were being caught up by the illness and death. They were being asked to grow up before their time, to become caregivers when they themselves needed care. Throughout this time, as the government failed to resolve these issues, Jacob and his colleagues steadfastly offered support and advocacy to those in need. Their work remains important. There is nothing so tragic as seeing a child stripped of his or her childhood. Ubuntu Education Fund helps children reclaim some of the freedom and joy that comes from knowing that you have someone to rely on, someone to help you face difficult tasks, to listen to your deepest fears, to share in the pleasure of learning and to revel in the delight of play."

—Archbishop Desmond Tutu

took me to a township called the White Location on account of all the zinc in the area. Wherever we looked, there were fires, and in front of each fire were little kids holding bricks. They were heating these bricks in order to iron their school uniforms. They looked so dignified and proud to be going to school. I looked at Banks and said, "We've got to do something to help these kids."

Ubuntu in Action

I went back to school and immediately went to see Dr. Berry, to tell her I didn't want to take classes anymore. I was just not good at sitting in class—it wasn't my thing. She was great about it. She said, "Okay, I'm going to put my neck on the line, but don't screw me over." I took independent studies with her.

With Dr. Berry's help and advice, I founded Ubuntu. It was a real shoe-string operation. I held a raffle and raised three hundred dollars. I put signs around campus, advertising meetings about the organization. At the sec-

ond meeting only one person showed. She turned out to be my future wife, Lindsay. After I graduated, I drove to the Arctic Ocean with a friend for two months. I drafted the whole business plan for Ubuntu in the wilderness.

In 1999 I went back to South Africa. Banks and I went on a shopping spree for school supplies with the small amount of money I had raised. We had our moments of doubt. I remember that after a week we just looked at each other and said, "What did we just do? This is a disaster. It isn't going to change anything." But we hung in there.

Banks and I spent six months going door-to-door, talking with everyone in the community: parents, teachers, students... anyone. We drew a seven-kilometer radius around us and decided that we wouldn't work outside this geographical region. We also decided we were going to only work with young children who had been sexually abused or raped, orphaned, or were HIV positive—the bottom of the bottom. We would invest in these kids every day of their lives. In the nonprofit world, everyone's obsessed with how much money they spend. I said, "No, that's bullshit. We're gonna spend as much as possible on each of these kids to get a level playing field."

Over the last thirteen years I have never stopped hustling. Sometimes you feel you are just playing catch-up. But eventually you learn what works. Three years ago our first nineteen kids went to university. Within two months, twelve of the nineteen failed out. We realized our goal wasn't to get them *into* university but *through* university. Just one year later we put 102 kids into university, and all 102 passed their first year on full scholarship.

A year ago we opened the Ubuntu Centre. The idea was to build something as nice as the nicest private school in Manhattan. It turned out to be a complex that cost seven million dollars, which in South Africa is a fortune.

The Power of Determination

I'm totally addicted to the challenge of building our programs. It is one thing to build a business. But try building it in a township with 90 percent unemployment, little infrastructure, halfway around the world from where your family lives.

I was a long-haired twenty-one-year-old with this crazy idea, surrounded by chaos and people telling me I couldn't do it. I like to prove people wrong.

I sleep four hours a night but I'm fine. It's a lifestyle. Too many of us are just floating through, ignoring what's around us. The hardest thing is taking that first step. If I'm on a plane, I'm gonna talk to the person next to me, because you don't know: Maybe they'll become the next donor. You have to be passionate about it.

This is hard stuff. There are challenges every day. It takes sustained intervention, the recruitment and development of talented people, investing in staff, the training of teachers, and building capacity all the time. We need to get better at what we do and support the next level of leadership. As we

The Ubuntu Centre is a dramatic architectural statement that, in the words of its designer, Stan Field, "allows the community to see themselves in an entirely different way." Constructed of natural and local materials and powered by solar and wind energy, the Centre represents a dramatic affirmation of purpose and connection. It houses a pediatric HIV clinic, a community theater, an education wing, and office space, as well as a rooftop vegetable garden.

get bigger, we have to systematize what we do without becoming a bureaucracy. To succeed you need to find your passion, be patient, hold yourself and others to high expectations, and define success by the quality of the intervention.

We're as flawed as the next group. It's taken years to find out what we're good at and what we are not good at. It has not been an easy journey. But, at the end of the day, it's the kids that keep us going—the kids at the bottom of the bottom who just need a chance and a level playing field. There is nothing more sustainable than investing in a kid every day of their lives. **"**

TO LEARN MORE ABOUT UBUNTU
EDUCATION FUND
please visit:

>Ubuntu Education Fund
www.ubuntufund.org

PO Box 14526
Sidwell 6061
Port Elizabeth
South Africa

OTHER ORGANIZATIONS EDUCATING
CHILDREN IN AFRICA:

>Africare
www.africare.org

Africare House
440 R Street NW
Washington, DC 20001

>Children's Movement
www.childrensmovement.org.za

3 Milner Road
Rondebosch, 7700
Cape Town
South Africa

>Cross-Cultural Solutions
www.crossculturalsolutions.org

2 Clinton Place
New Rochelle, NY 10801

>UNICEF South Africa
www.unicef.org

PO Box 4884
Pretoria, 0001
South Africa

IT'S A
SACRED OBLIGATION

the
Nate Fick
story

CHIEF EXECUTIVE OFFICER, THE CENTER FOR A NEW AMERICAN SECURITY

NATE FICK'S STORY IS ESPECIALLY CLOSE TO MY HEART. Like my son, Zach, Nate was a Marine officer. He served in both the Iraq and Afghanistan wars. Talking to Nate, I could sense the enormous toll war takes on the minds and souls of the courageous young men and women who serve our country in the military. The lucky ones, like Nate and Zach, have found ways to reconcile conflicting feelings about their wartime experiences. Nate wrote a wonderful book, *One Bullet Away: The Making of a Marine Officer*. My son chose to produce, write, and direct a film, *The Western Front*.

After graduating from the Kennedy School of Government at Harvard, Nate became CEO at the Center for a New American Security (CNAS), an independent, nonpartisan research institution established in 2007 by Kurt Campbell (an American diplomat and currently Assistant Secretary of State for East Asian and Pacific Affairs) and Michele Flournoy (who, until very recently, was the Under Secretary of Defense for Policy). In his position as CEO, Nate leads others as they delve into the nation's most significant military issues and problems, helping to shape the national security policies that affect not only our troops but each and every one of us every day.

THE SUFFERING CAUSED BY WAR IS STAGGERING. The Institute for Economics and Peace estimates that a 25 percent increase in world peacefulness would increase economic productivity by seven trillion dollars—to say nothing about the untold number of lives that would be saved. But conflict cannot be wished away. It needs to be eliminated though policies and practices that can lead enemies to look beyond their differences and find common ground.

Based in Washington, D.C., CNAS engages policymakers, experts, and the public with innovative, fact-based research, ideas, and analyses. The areas they work in include cybersecurity, defense spending, diplomacy, economic development, security issues in Afghanistan and Pakistan, developing civilian capacity, energy security, and climate change.

The heart of the Nate Fick story, however, isn't about policies or white papers; it is about integrity, courage, compassion, and a profound decency. Rudy Reyes wrote this about his commanding officer when he reviewed *One Bullet Away*: "A Recon Marine always gives more than he takes. With this said, I respectfully thank and honor Capt. Fick for his private and revealing book about idealism, loss of innocence, and the Mask of Command. Do leaders regret, do they feel, do they disagree? Yes, the legit ones do. *One Bullet Away* reveals Fick's secret heart and the violence it bears and also the man's truth and compassion gained by combat."

This is a story of a young American who, through the inferno of war, was forged into a leader for the twenty-first century.

The Making of a Marine

"I grew up in Baltimore, the son of a self-employed lawyer and a social worker. I would describe my parents as very compassionate, engaged people who care about their community. They were a real influence on me and my two younger sisters. We are not a military family, but my dad served for a couple of years. It was kind of the classic story. Dad was a self-described screwup—he had the wild edge—and the Army sort of beat him straight. He went from there to law school and then on with the rest of his life.

I graduated from Dartmouth in 1999 and intended to go to med school, but I gradually realized I only wanted to go because other people told me I should. It didn't arise from anything inside of me. So I started to look for another path.

The Marines have a summer program called the Platoon Leaders Course, where you go for ten weeks. If you graduate, you can either accept your commission and go on and serve as an officer, or you can walk away and say, "Hey thanks, guys, this was great, but it's not for me."

I was certainly inspired by my dad. I was also inspired by studying the classics in college. In the classical world, there was the notion that to be a productive citizen you have to give something back. It can take many forms, but the classical one for young men in the ancient world was military service. And then there was the reality that I wanted to travel, to work outdoors—and I liked the cool technology. I was seduced by the Marine recruiting commercials.

When I headed off to the Marines, my dad said something to me that I didn't appreciate at the time and took me a decade to understand: "The Marines will teach you everything I love you too much to teach you." He was right.

Our JFK Moment

I spent two years in the peacetime military. We were training with the Australian Army in northern Australia on September 11, 2001. The next morning we were on our way to the coast of Pakistan. We felt anger, fear, and a sense of vulnerability. But we were not impotent, we were not passive. There was this overwhelming sense of purpose and unity around a cause, a feeling that I had never experienced before in my life.

My future wife, Margaret, was on a bus in New York City on 9/11. She moved from finance to public education because she started rethinking her personal priorities. My parents talked about their JFK moment: November 22, 1963. September 11, 2001, was ours.

My unit spent the fall and winter of 2002 in Afghanistan and Pakistan; I went to Iraq in the spring of 2003. In Afghanistan I appreciated the overwhelming sense of mission that unified us all. But when it came to the war in Iraq, opinions in our unit spanned the spectrum of opinion in the United States. I have moderate DNA. Even so, I didn't see the link between Al Qaeda and the Hussein regime. I didn't spend as much time reflecting on it as I probably should have.

At the end of those conversations, we put away our personal opinions,

because we had sworn an oath under the Constitution to obey the lawful orders of a democratically elected government. None of us wants to live in a society where the guys with the guns are the ones making the decisions, and that really puts the burden of responsibility on the political leadership to do the right thing.

In January 2003 we were dropped in the desert of northern Kuwait. All of a sudden we were isolated; we were in a vacuum. The only link to the outside world was a hand-cranked Grundig shortwave radio, a throwback to the 1930s. I was the leader of a twenty-five-Marine reconnaissance unit. Our mission was critically important to the success of the invasion because we were one of the forward units; we were out in front.

The Sacred Geometry of Chance

Many Marines I knew were killed, although none of them were in my command. That achievement had nothing to do with me—war is capricious. In a conversation I witnessed between two commanders, one argued that the other was not aggressive enough. The guy being accused said, "You wouldn't feel that way if you had a child." Those words have always stuck with me.

One of my most treasured memories was talking with one of my Marines on the morning after we were ambushed by a group of Syrians. One of the lead Marines was shot, and Rudy Reyes had to step up and take over. Rudy grew up in west Texas, an orphan. He was sent to a series of state-run orphanages, which he describes as "gladiator academies." He hadn't gone to college. Rudy's one of the people who have really driven home to me the point that education and intelligence are not correlated.

As the sun was coming up, I found Rudy holding an AK-47 bullet in his hand. It was the bullet that had passed through the team leader and then rattled to a stop inside the Humvee. I asked, "How are you doing, Rudy?"

and he said, "The difference between life and death out here is seconds and millimeters. It's the sacred geometry of chance."

At the end of the day, I had two litmus tests that any mission had to pass before I would sign off on it. I would not ask my Marines to do something that was morally unjustifiable, and if somebody got killed, I needed to be able to sit down in the living room with his mother and father to explain to them why their son was killed working for me—and why I had thought it was worth it.

That sets the bar so high. But you clear it. You clear it every day.

It's a Sacred Obligation

My time in Iraq was fairly brief. The invasion began in March 2003, and I came home in June of that same year. At that time we were winning the wars in both Afghanistan and Iraq. If you had told me a decade later we would still be engaged in both places, I wouldn't have believed it.

I got out of the service in early 2004. I was going to rotate to a desk job, but I decided to get out instead. Joining the Marines was the best decision I could have made, and getting out was the second-best decision. It was time for me to go. I didn't have the constitution that really successful officers have.

I am cut from a slightly different cloth. I had read in college about the great Roman warrior Cincinnatus, who famously put down his plow for the sword and then put down his sword to return to the plow. It was time for me to return to my plow.

"I myself was one bullet away on more than one occasion, and in one particular ambush Capt. Fick laid it on the line and decisively and calmly saved my team's life. I will always admire, respect, and love the warrior who gave more than he took from 1st Recon Battalion. And his men are of the same mind as myself." —Rudy Reyes

But the transition back to civilian life was brutally hard. Part of it was the wonders of modern transportation. I left Afghanistan on a ship, and it took a month and a half to get home. I left Iraq on a jet and within two days went from wearing body armor and carrying a gun to having dinner on the beach with my parents in San Diego.

At the end of this very awkward meal, where we were all talking past each other, a good friend finally said, "So how was the war?" I said, "Fine," and went back to eating my dinner. I mean, you couldn't convey it.

My family was really worried about me. The guy that followed me in command of my platoon was killed in April 2004. The war was getting worse every week. So I decided to write, because I could write things that I couldn't talk about. The process was totally cathartic, but the manuscript was rejected by twenty-five publishers. Eventually I found an agent, and all of a sudden some publishers were interested.

I then went to the Kennedy School of Government. On the first day, I sat down next to a woman named Margaret. We said hello, but I thought we had nothing in common. We started running together. I thought I was in pretty good shape, but she had just returned from the Olympic Trials in Athens, and she quickly put me in my place. That was in the fall of 2004. We got married in the fall of 2007.

Margaret is from the Upper East Side in New York City. I joke with her that the only man in uniform she had ever seen before me was the doorman of her apartment building. She doesn't think it's funny.

Margaret saved me—by loving me. We have two daughters, Ella, who was born in March 2010, and Kate, who was born in March 2012. In the spring

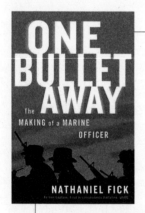

"I left the Corps because I had become a reluctant warrior. Many Marines reminded me of gladiators. They had that mysterious quality that allows some men to strap on greaves and a breastplate and wade into the gore. I respected, admired, and emulated them, but I could never be like them. I could kill when killing was called for, and I got hooked on the rush of combat as much as any man did. But I couldn't make the conscious choice to put myself in that position again and again throughout my professional life. Great Marine commanders, like all great warriors, are able to kill that which they love most—their men. It's a fundamental law of warfare. Twice I had cheated it. I couldn't tempt fate again."

—Nate Fick, *One Bullet Away*

of 2010, President Obama gave a speech about Iraq and said it was time to turn the page. I couldn't agree more; it's time to turn the page. Let's get on with it.

Eventually the siren song of the policy world lured me back. Michele Flournoy invited me to join a new national-security think tank, CNAS. President Obama chose Michele to be the U.S. undersecretary of defense for policy, and I became the CEO of CNAS. It feels like a natural progression to me. It's very humbling when you realize that the things you write matter, that people listen. It means you had better get it right. If you do your homework, it is very fulfilling.

It has been enormously gratifying to watch this start-up mature into a more stable, professional, "all-weather" institution. I've learned that my role isn't to get elbows-deep in policy work, but rather to focus on finding the best talent, fostering a culture and workplace that helps them do their best, and then provide the needed resources. Every now and then—in moments of crisis— I find myself reaching back to my earliest training and experience as a Marine officer when personal leadership is required. There is no substitute for looking people in the eye and saying, "Okay, here's what we need to do, and we'll do it together."

The main challenge for American security today is to establish some consensus on the role of American power and purpose in this century. Twenty years after the end of the cold war, we are pulling our heads up and asking who we are and what world we want to live in. Answering those questions and putting in place the relationships and the doctrine that keep answering them is the most fundamental challenge of American national security.

One of my favorite quotes is from John Adams: "I must study politics and war that my sons may have liberty to study math and philosophy." Our children should live without conflict and war. There are a lot of good people I knew in the service who either didn't come home or who came home fundamentally changed.

We have a duty to take what we saw and what we learned and try to make sure the same mistakes don't happen again. To preserve what was good—a sense of purpose, unity, and justice: Make that the hallmark of whatever we do.

It's a sacred obligation. "

TO LEARN MORE ABOUT THE CENTER FOR
A NEW AMERICAN SECURITY
please visit:

>Center for a New American Security
www.cnas.org
1301 Pennsylvania Avenue NW (Suite 403)
Washington, DC 20004

OTHER ORGANIZATIONS SPECIALIZING IN
FOREIGN POLICY AND NATIONAL SECURITY:

>Council on Foreign Relations
www.cfr.org
1777 F Street NW
Washington, DC 20006

>Foreign Policy Association
www.fpa.org
470 Park Avenue South
New York, NY 10016

>United States Institute of Peace
www.usip.org
2301 Constitution Avenue NW
Washington, DC 20037

>World Affairs Councils of America
www.worldaffairscouncils.org
1200 18th Street NW (Suite 902)
Washington, DC 20036

Afterword: Turning Points

WHEN I WAS IN HIGH SCHOOL, Ruth Klein, one of our most respected teachers, addressed the student body a few days after John F. Kennedy was assassinated. She concluded her moving talk with these words: "For the death of our young president is at once the salty taste of 'the tears for human beings' of which the poet Virgil spoke, and a reminder that we—the old that teach you—trust you—the young who learn—to light the fire that may kindle a better world."

I hope that *Hearts on Fire* has kindled your fire to make a better world and connect you to your sense of purpose. Each of us in our own unique way has a role to play in actively making a more just and equitable world. There are so many ways to give back; whatever your chosen field, you can contribute to and share in the excitement of the movement to create a more engaged, concerned, compassionate, and passionate global citizenry. *Hearts on Fire* is meant to jump-start your own quest to ignite idealism into action.

What are some of the qualities of those who turn good intentions into good work? Certainly, they combine an excellence in effort and performance with an ethic of fairness; they exemplify commitment and humility; and they are relentless in their pursuit of finding grassroots solutions to the complex problems of the twenty-first century.

Visionaries don't wait for others to step forward and take action. They walk the walk. They step out. They are brave. And they connect with others in deep and real ways.

Often, a life of purposeful action begins with a decisive turning point—think of Amy recuperating after the operation on her shoulder, Jimmie interviewing rape victims in Africa, Maria handing a baby killed by war to its mother, Jacob witnessing poverty-stricken children in South Africa iron their school clothes with hot bricks, Sara reconnecting to her union roots, Nate recognizing the human cost of war, and Leila tutoring the blind and brilliant Femi Abbas.

These moments of deep understanding become turning points, redirecting a life and setting into motion a life's work. For some, the turning point happens in a flash, but for others it comes gradually, along a winding road with many detours—yet somehow each individual's passion for righting wrongs keeps him or her moving in the direction of overcoming challenges and finding a way to success.

Most of the visionaries we have met in these pages did not grow up with any special privileges—some grew up in difficult circumstances—but when they encountered dire hardship, all of them were struck by a sense of their own privilege...and a new purpose. Think of Josh, Isaac, and Nadim seeing the need for basic medical care for all, Susana putting her college education to work for environmental justice in California, Andeisha reaching out to the poorest of Afghan children, Diahann forgoing a profitable career in the law to undertake a life of service, and Vivian tutoring women in prison.

In the fourteenth century the mystic Catherine of Siena once said, "If you are what you should be, you will set the whole world on fire." The message of visionaries is "Be what you should be, become committed to your calling, and you will set the world on fire." Not everyone needs to travel to Africa or other faraway places to light the world on fire; we can follow Catherine's exhortation right here at home.

We are living at the beginning of a great turning point in history, and each and every person has a right to be part of it. In my 2009 note to self, I asked if we are at a tipping point where the horrors of the past are being replaced with collaborative efforts. I feel confident the answer is yes. One of the messages I draw from knowing people of vision is their deep belief in individual agency and collective action. "Love thy neighbor as thyself" is not just a nice phrase; it is a living principle of daily life.

And who is our neighbor? Is it the person next door or the child halfway around the world? In today's world the answer is both—we need to connect with those closest to us and we need to connect with those we will never see in person but with whom we share the earth's fate. The understanding that we are our brothers'—and sisters'—keepers opens us up to a life that is alive with opportunity and action. To see the world afresh every day with possibility is the spark that turns ashes into hearts on fire.

What better way to live than with a heart on fire for justice and fairness for all?

Jill W. Iscol
July 2011

Resources

IN 2011, THE ECHOING GREEN FOUNDATION published a very useful book, *Work on Purpose*. In the "Resources" section, authors Lara Galinsky and Kelly Nuxoll have compiled an extensive list of resources for anyone who wants to know more about the world of service and social innovation; to learn more, please visit their website: www.echoinggreen.org.

Our website—www.heartsonfirebook.com—is a growing resource for those seeking more information about how visionaries are turning idealism into action. Please join us.

Below are a number of organizations offering resources to individuals with bold ideas about how to change the world for the better.

>Acumen Fund
www.acumenfund.org
76 Ninth Avenue (Suite 315)
New York, NY 10011

>Ashoka: Innovators for the Public
www. ashoka.org
1700 North Moore Street
Arlington, VA 22209

>City Year
www.cityyear.org
287 Columbus Avenue
Boston, MA 02116

>Clinton Global Initiative University
www.cgiu.org
1301 Avenue of the Americas (37th Floor)
New York, NY 10019

>Community Wealth Ventures, Inc.
www.communitywealth.com
1825 K Street NW
Washington, DC 20006

>Coro Fellows Program
www.coro.org
700 12th Street, NW (Suite 1100)
Washington, DC 20005

>Echoing Green Foundation
www. echoinggreen.org
198 Madison Avenue (8th Floor)
New York, NY 10016

>Skoll Foundation
www.skollfoundation.org
250 University Avenue (Suite 200)
Palo Alto, CA 94301

>Surdna Foundation
www.surdna.org
330 Madison Avenue (30th Floor)
New York, NY 10017

>The Petra Foundation
www.petrafoundation.org
315 Duke Ellington Blvd. (Suite 16C)
New York, NY 10025

Further Reading

BELOW IS A SELECTED READING LIST that is by no means comprehensive but can serve as a starting place for those interested in learning more about how individuals and groups are changing the world for the better.

Bornstein, David. 2004. *How to Change the World: Social Entrepreneurs and the Power of New Ideas*. New York: Oxford University Press.

Clinton, Bill. 2007. *Giving: How Each of Us Can Change the World*. New York: Alfred A. Knopf.

Collier, Paul. 2007. *The Bottom Billion: Why the Poorest Countries Are Failing and What Can Be Done About It*. Oxford, UK: Oxford University Press.

Crutchfield, Leslie R., and Heather McLeod Grant. 2007. *Forces for Good: The Six Practices of High-Impact Nonprofits*. San Francisco: Jossey-Bass.

Galinsky, Lara, and Kelly Nuxoll. 2011. *Work on Purpose*. New York: Echoing Green.

Gardner, Howard, Mihaly Csikszentmihalyi, and William Damon. 2001. *Good Work: When Excellence and Ethics Meet*. New York: Basic Books.

Gladwell, Malcolm. 2000. *The Tipping Point: How Little Things Can Make a Big Difference*. New York: Little, Brown.

Hawken, Paul. 2007. *Blessed Unrest: How the Largest Social Movement in History Is Restoring Grace, Justice, and Beauty to the World*. New York: Viking.

Lemmon, Gayle Tzemach. 2011. *The Dressmaker of Khair Khana*. New York: HarperCollins Publishers.

Novogratz, Jacqueline. 2009. *The Blue Sweater: Bridging the Gap Between Rich and Poor in an Interconnected World*. New York: Rodale.

Olberding, John C., and Lisa Barnwell Williams, eds. 2010. *Building Strong Nonprofits: New Strategies for Growth and Sustainability*. Hoboken, NJ: John Wiley & Sons.

Pogge, Thomas. 2008. *World Poverty and Human Rights*. Cambridge, UK: Polity Press.

Sachs, Jeffery D. 2005. *The End of Poverty: Economic Possibilities for Our Time*. New York: Penguin.

Sen, Amartya. 1999. *Development as Freedom*. New York: Alfred A. Knopf.

Shiva, Vandana. 2002. *Water Wars: Privatization, Pollution, and Profit*. Cambridge, MA: South End Press.

Shore, Bill. 1999. *The Cathedral Within: Transforming Your Life by Giving Something Back*. New York: Random House.

Welch, Wilford. 2008. *The Tactics of Hope: How Social Entrepreneurs Are Changing the World*. San Rafael, CA: Earth Aware Editions.

Weston, Anthony. 2007. *How to Re-Imagine the World: A Pocket Guide for Practical Visionaries*. Gabriola Island, CN: New Society Publishers.

Yunus, Muhammad. 2007. *Creating a World Without Poverty: Social Business and the Future of Capitalism*. New York: Public Affairs.

Acknowledgments

I WILL ALWAYS BE GRATEFUL to the many friends and mentors who have helped enrich my life professionally and personally:

Gary Simons, Prep for Prep; Jonah Edelman, Stand for Children; Margot Strom, Facing History and Ourselves; Billy Shore, Share Our Strength; the team at City Year New York—Ken Grouf, Mithra Ramaley, Itai Dinour, David Caplan and Jack Lew; CY's founders, Alan Khazei and Michael Brown; and Sal La Spada, CEO of the Philanthropy Workshop.

Also Alyse Nelson, Ambassador Melanne Verveer, Baroness Mary Goudie, Stephenie Foster, Lorie Jackson, Kathy Hendrix, Melysa Sperber, Celena Green, and Helah Robinson of Vital Voices Global Partnership, as well as the remarkable women who comprised VVGP's Africa Advisory Council: Dr. Ngozi Okonjo Iweala, Kah Walla, Zoe Dean-Smith, Hafsat Abiola-Costello, Vongai Chikwanda, Annie Rashidi Mulumba, Hilary Gbedemah, Eva Muraya, Abby Onencan Muricho, Dr. Kakenya Ntaiya, Phyllis Mwangi, Gina Barbieri, Theo Sowa, and Dawn Marole.

Without the help of Cheryl Dorsey, CEO of Echoing Green, Penny Abeywardena, who also advised me to write this book as a Clinton Global Initiative (CGI) commitment, and Meg Fidler, CEO of the Petra Foundation, I would never have met the extraordinary visionaries in *Hearts on Fire*. I only wish I could have included everyone they recommended.

I am especially grateful to Jacqueline Novogratz, founder and CEO of the Acumen Fund, for teaching me that, yes, in fact, it is okay to talk about morality, goodness, love, and the ability for all of us to help build a world we had all imagined.

The seeds of inspiration for this book were sown more than a decade ago, during the three years I chaired the Family Reunion Conference, founded and moderated by then vice president Al Gore and Tipper Gore. It is because of this experience that my husband, Ken, and I launched and endowed the Iscol Family Program for Leadership Development at Cornell University in 2001. I am indebted to Professor John Eckenrode and his team—Jan Conrad and Patricia Thayer—for turning this idea into a reality and for valuing visionaries the way we do.

Many thanks to Cathee Weiss for her early mentorship; also thanks to

Peter Osnos for suggesting that we self-publish and for introducing us to Della Mancuso—and to Della for keeping the project on track, watching my back as we navigated through the new world of self-publishing, and bringing on board Mary Kornblum, our fabulously talented book designer, and Rick Ball, our meticulous copy editor…and to Zac Adam Cohen, our Web designer.

Without the energy and insight of our publicist, Lisa Weinert, I would be still wondering how to get the word out about *Hearts on Fire*. (And thanks to Lisa Witter for introducing me to someone so committed to this work.)

My agent Jesseca Salky, founding partner of HSG Agency, had total faith in *Hearts on Fire* from the very beginning and was an indispensible guide, colleague, and friend as I made my way through the world of publishing for the first time. Her steady hand and clear thinking brought it all together.

The team at Random House has been superb. The spirited support and enthusiasm of publisher Jane von Mehren, director of publicity Sally Marvin, and publicist Michelle Jasmine have made the publication of *Hearts on Fire* a wonderful experience. I am particularly indebted to our editor Ben Steinberg for his expertise and utter commitment to the message, power, and poetry of the visionaries. He is the best editor a writer could ask for.

Also on the team were my dear friends John Dauer, a visual visionary who produced and directed all the website videos, and the brilliant Pat Dauer, who not only wrote the website videos and provided editorial advice on every aspect of this project, but who was also always the consummate professional, bringing her considerable talent and expertise to guide me through the most challenging parts of this project; and my incredibly dedicated and capable assistant, Sara Arlotti, who went beyond the call of duty, devoting endless hours and unflagging attention to all the thousands of details.

This book would never have been realized had it not been for the complete dedication of my friend and co-author, Peter Cookson. With grace, generosity, and wisdom, he made *Hearts on Fire* as beautiful as it is because he cared deeply about the project and became as committed and inspired as

I am by the visionaries, their work, and their personal stories. His organizational skills provided the scaffolding my team and I needed as we joined the burgeoning self-publishing sector.

I have been deeply influenced by both President Bill Clinton and Secretary of State Hillary Clinton. Their lives truly capture the essence of what it means to use all of one's talents and gifts to improve the lives of others. Their ethic of service and their compassion for all humanity continues to be an inspiration to me. I am honored to count them among my dear friends.

My indispensable cheerleaders throughout this project have been, as always, my sisters, Faith Drucker and Beth Sperber; my nieces, Amy Drucker—who contributed to the book jacket photos—Melysa Sperber, another brilliant visionary who is dedicating her life to combating violence against women, including sex trafficking; Kim Sperber and Valerie Hepner; and my nephews, Adam Drucker and James Hepner; and so many friends, including Terry Blumenfeld, Toni Sosnoff, Joanna Cole, Kathy Kauff, Carrie Odell, Suzanne Kayne, and Linda Fairstein. They provided thoughtful input and helped me get over the emotional roadblocks that otherwise might have sidetracked this journey.

I owe so much to my beloved parents, Milton Weinick and Sylvia Schaefer (née Friedman), who conveyed to me and my sisters that to whom much is given much is expected. I was blessed by seeing them treat others with the dignity they believed all people deserve.

And I've saved the best for last...the three pillars on whom all my dreams and successes stand. The first two are my children, Zachary and Kiva, whose insights and love are pure and priceless. They have always been my best teachers. By observing them take on their own tough challenges, they have given me courage to do the same.

And the third pillar is my fiercest supporter, my husband, Ken. His encouragement, love, and admiration inspired me to go forward with *Hearts on Fire*. That he, too, fell in love with the visionaries—and thinks we should tell the stories of others like them—is the best tribute to the impact of *Hearts on Fire*. He is my anchor.

Photo Credits and Text Permissions

Cover (Go! Ubuntu! Go! photo):
David Keyes

Pages ix, 118 and cover, 153: © 2011 Amy Drucker for Soulshine Imagery

Pages 1, 4, 9 (bottom) and cover:
Damaso Reyes

Page 3: Leah Overstreet

Page 9 (top): © Christophe Calais/Corbis

Page 9: Excerpt from A Letter to My Daughter reprinted with permission from Jimmie Briggs

Page 11 (left): © Panmela Castro

Page 11 (right): © Jenna Arnold

Pages 15, 19 and cover, 22 and cover:
Damian Drake

Page 16: © Satellite and Aerial/age footstock

Pages 17, 18: Joel Frushone

Page 27 and cover (photo of Josh Nesbit), 31 (top): Casey Nesbit

Page 27 and cover (photo of Nadim Mahmud), 35: Michael Nedelman and David Tracey

Page 27 and cover (photo of Isaac Holeman): © 2010 Tony Deifell

Pages 28–29: Isaac Holeman

Page 30: Ryan Gonzalez

Pages 32, 33 and cover: Photos courtesy of Isaac Holeman

Page 34: Alex Harsha

Page 36: Photo courtesy of Nadim Mahmud

Pages 41, 44, 45, 48: Erin Lubin

Pages 42–43 and cover: Roberto Guerra

Page 47 and cover: Photo courtesy of Community Water Center

Pages 51, 54 and cover, 56 (left and right), 57 (top and bottom): Farid Ahmad Alami

Page 52: © Olira/Dreamstime.com

Page 53: Andeisha Farid

Pages 61 and cover, 63, 65, 67 (left and right), 70 (top, middle, and bottom):
Ved Chirayath

Page 62: © Youssouf Cader/Dreamstime.com

Page 69: Nobel Peace Prize Lecture © Nobel Foundation

Pages 73 and cover, 76, 80 and cover: Photos courtesy of New York City Mayor's Office

Page 74: © images4/Fotolia.com

Page 75: © SeanPavonePhoto/Fotolia.com

Page 78: Photo courtesy of Diahann Billings-Burford

Pages 83 and cover, 85, 86, 88, 90, 91 (left and right): Hugo Cabrera for Kiej de los Bosques

Page 84: © Olira/Dreamstime.com

Page 89: © palou/Fotolia.com

Pages 95, 98 and cover, 100: Photos courtesy of Freelancers Union

Pages 96, 101, 102: Images reprinted with permission from Freelancers Union

Page 97: © Daniel Arnold

Pages 105 and cover, 108: Larry Bercow

Page 106: Image reprinted with permission from College and Community Fellowship

Page 107: © Aaron Kohr/Fotolia.com

Page 110: © Patrick Egan/City Limits

Page 111: Margot Jordan

Page 112 (left): Starlene Patterson

Page 112 (right): Karl Crutchfield

Pages 115, 120 and cover (photo of girl writing): Vance Jacobs

Page 116: © Ingvar Bjork

Pages 117, 122, 124: Jess Field

Page 119: Spencer Gordon

Pages 119, 121: Excerpts from "I Am Because You Are" (working title) reprinted with permission from Jacob Lief

Pages 127, 130 and cover: Liz Lynch

Page 128: © zorani/istock.com

Pages 129, 132: Photos courtesy of Nathaniel Fick

Pages 133, 134: Image and excerpts from One Bullet Away reprinted with permission from Nathaniel Fick

Index

Page numbers in *italics* refer to illustrations.

About the Authors

EDUCATOR AND ACTIVIST Jill Iscol, EdD, is president of the IF Hummingbird Foundation, a family foundation established in 1989 to support domestic and international efforts to strengthen democracy and reduce the social, economic, and educational inequalities that threaten it. Jill began her career as a public school teacher in New York City and has continued her lifelong commitment to education through her active involvement with the Bank Street College of Education and Teachers College, Columbia University. For the past two decades Jill has developed an expertise in identifying visionary leaders and programs at early stages of their development. She fosters their advancement by providing seed capital and guidance, enabling them to become stable, sustainable, and successful organizations, impacting lives around the globe. In the past these organizations have included Prep for Prep, Stand for Children, Facing History and Ourselves, and Vital Voices Global Partnership. They currently include Acumen Fund, where she serves as a founding advisory board member; City Year New York, of which she was a founding co-chair; and the Iscol Family Program for Leadership Development at Cornell University.

Jill has been actively involved in the Democratic Party and served as chairperson of the Annual Family Re-Union Conference, moderated by Vice President Gore and Mrs. Gore. She also served as co-chair for Hillary Rodham Clinton for Senate's New York finance committee and as national vice-chair of Hillary Rodham Clinton for President's 2008 finance committee.

Most recently, Jill serves as a trustee of Horizons National, on the advisory board of the Center for New American Security in Washington and as a member of the New York State Commission on National and Community Service, and in 2011 was appointed to the US-Afghan Women's Council.

Jill received a bachelor of arts, magna cum laude, from University of Pittsburgh (1967), a doctorate from Teachers College, Columbia University (1976), and a master of philosophy in sociology from Yale University (1990).

SOCIOLOGIST, AUTHOR, AND EDUCATIONAL REFORMER Peter W. Cookson, Jr., PhD, is the founder of Ideas without Borders, an educational consulting firm based in Washington, D.C., specializing in twenty-first-century education and human rights. His experience with social entrepreneurship began in the mid-1990s, when he founded and led the Center for Educational Outreach and Innovation at Teachers College, Columbia University. Peter is currently a member of the Department of Educational Policy and Social Analysis at Teachers College and Senior Fellow at Education Sector in Washington, D.C.

He is the author or co-author of fifteen books, including *Preparing for Power: America's Elite Boarding Schools, Expect Miracles: Charter Schools and the Politics of Hope and Despair, Making Sense of Society, School Choice: The Struggle for the Soul of American Education,* and *Sacred Trust: A Children's Education Bill of Rights.*

His work has been favorably reviewed in *The New York Times, The Washington Post, Publishers Weekly, Kirkus Reviews, Harvard Educational Review, Newsweek, U.S. News & World Report, Child, Success,* and *Woman's Day.* He has appeared on WWOR-TV, ABC-TV, Fox Cable Network News, and PBS.

Peter is a featured speaker at numerous international and national meetings and is currently undertaking a national public engagement campaign in conjunction with the release of *Sacred Trust.*

He received a bachelor of arts (1966), master of arts (1968), and doctorate (1981) from New York University. He holds a certificate of advanced study from the Harvard Graduate School of Education (1991) and a master of arts in religion from Yale University (2010).